CAST IRON
AUTOMOTIVE TOYS

Myra Yellin Outwater & Eric B. Outwater
Stevie & Bill Weart

4880 Lower Valley Road, Atglen, PA 19310 USA

Dedication

To all those collectors, who through their collections, have saved so much of our cultural history, and to our fathers who shared with us their love for the automobile.

Acknowledgments

David Bausch
Richard Dent
Charles Schalebaum
Thank you for all your help!
Myra & Eric Outwater

Library of Congress Cataloging-in-Publication Data

Outwater, Myra Yellin.
    Cast iron automotive toys/ Myra Yellin Outwater & Eric B. Outwater.
      p. cm.
    ISBN 0-7643-1077-1
    1. Automobiles--Models--Collectors and collecting--United States--Catalogs. 2. Metal toys--Collectors and collecting--United States--Catalogs. 3. Cast iron--Collectors and collecting--United States--Catalogs. I. Outwater, Eric Boe. II. Title.
    TL237.2.O88 2000
    629.22'1'074--dc21   99-059468

Designed by "Sue"
Type set in AmericanaXBd BT/Humanst521 BT
ISBN: 0-7643-1077-1
Printed in China
1 2 3 4

Published by Schiffer Publishing Ltd.
4880 Lower Valley Road
Atglen, PA 19310
Phone: (610) 593-1777; Fax: (610) 593-2002
E-mail: Schifferbk@aol.com
Please visit our web site catalog at **www.schifferbooks.com**
We are always looking for people to write books on new and related subjects. If you have an idea for a book, please contact us at the above address.

This book may be purchased from the publisher.
Include $3.95 for shipping.
Please try your bookstore first.
You may write for a free catalog.

In Europe, Schiffer books are distributed by:
Bushwood Books
6 Marksbury Ave.
Kew Gardens
Surrey TW9 4JF England
Phone: 44 (0)208 392-8585; Fax: 44 (0)208 392-9876
E-mail: Bushwd@aol.com
Free postage in the UK. Europe: air mail at cost.
Try your bookstore first.

Contents

Preface

We have often been asked, "Why did you write a book about automotive cast iron toys? And what do you know about the topic?"

In the beginning, we just answered, "We're from Allentown, Pennsylvania. Toys have always been part of the area culture." And in truth, since the late 1890s, the Allentown area has been an important hub for the antique and cast iron toy world. Within just a few miles of Allentown were the Dent Hardware Company in Fullerton, Shimer and Son in Freemansburg, and Jones & Bixler in Easton. And only an hour or so away was the Hubley Manufacturing Company in Lancaster. For more than two centuries, this area has had a long tradition of ingenuity and craftsmanship. Its largest ethnic group, the Pennsylvania Germans, were known for their fine artistry and produced many wonderful hand-carved wooden and intricate tin toys.

We have been on the periphery of the toy world for many years. Each fall we have wandered through the Allentown Toy Show at the Fairgrounds, attended Das Awkscht Fescht each August in nearby Macungie, and listened to friends recall the bounty of their trips to Renningers in Adamstown, Hershey, and Carlisle. Since the 1960s, the area has been attracting automotive toy collectors from all over the country. And today it is the home of many outstanding collectors such as David Bausch, Bill and Stevie Weart, Tom Sage, Charlie Schalebaum, as well as being known for more than two decades as the home of the Raymond E. Holland Automotive Art Collection.

The idea for doing this book came about while we were curating a show on antique cloth Advertising dolls at the Kemerer Museum of Decorative Arts in Bethlehem. While setting up our own show, we wandered into the adjoining gallery and saw the Kemerer's collection of Dent cast iron toys, a gift from Richard Dent, the grandson of the founder of the company.

In writing many books for Schiffer Publishing, we have become experts at finding experts. And before beginning any book, we search for outstanding collections and enlist the aid and expertise of those knowledgeable in the field. Through the years, we have met many kind people who have invited us into their homes, shared with us hospitality, knowledge, and enthusiasm, and allowed us to photograph their collections.

So when we decided to do this book, we immediately sought out an expert on cast iron toys, David Bausch. It was David who told us that one of the finest toy collections in the country was just a few miles away, and that's how we met Bill and Stevie Weart.

Working with the Wearts has been an extraordinary experience. For the past few months we have spent hours each week admiring and photographing their toys, researching their books, eating peanut butter on crackers, and immersing ourselves in the intricacies of cast iron toys.

Stevie and Bill have been collecting toys for more than twenty-eight years and have amassed one of the most comprehensive collections of American cast iron automotive toys in the country. Avid collectors and scholars, they spent months pouring through their extensive collection of catalogs to research the production periods of each toy pictured. Today, they are acknowledged experts in the field. All the cast iron toys pictured in this book come from the Wearts' personal collection.

Working on this book has brought back many memories for us. My "grownup" husband became a child again, as he paused in his photography to play with a toy. The Packards brought back memories of my grandfather sitting in his first car; the motorcycles brought back romantic memories of high school rides; and the milk and ice cream trucks brought back memories of lazy summer afternoons waiting for the ice cream man or early mornings waking up and finding milk bottles standing next to the door.

Recently Eric and I drove out west, racing through the prairies and badlands of North and South Dakota. As we passed rich fertile fields of wheat and soy beans, we saw (what we now know are) John Deere and McCormick-Deering tractors, hay mowers, disc harrows, and other farm equipment burrowing into the fields and stirring up clouds of dust from the harvest.

The cast iron toys in our book are not only beautiful and wonderfully made, but they are an important part of our American industrial history. These toys recall a simpler America, an American society that was half city and half farm. The days when these toys were first played with are long gone, with the memories slowly disappearing into the past. And we hope that our book and our collaboration with the Wearts will become an important part of the permanent record.

Myra Yellin Outwater & Eric B. Outwater
The Pondhouse, Center Valley, Pennsylvania
September 1999

Building A Collection:
A Toy Collector Looks Back

The toys in our collection bring back so many memories. Every time I look at them, I remember where they came from, when we bought them, and all the people and places we have come to know through the years.

Looking back I know I must have always been a toy collector at heart. As a child I collected and played with British Dinky toys, accumulating about 300 of them before I stopped collecting and began to save for my first "real" car.

Our present collection started in January of 1972 when we bought an Arcade Fordson tractor for $10 at a rundown flea market in Walled Lake, Michigan. That was our first cast iron toy purchase and we knew nothing about them.

Buying that first cast iron toy rekindled my own desire to collect toys, and this time I had a willing partner, my wife Stevie. Within a few months, we were spending weekends at antiques shows, car flea markets, and antiques shops.

It was at the Ann Arbor Antiques Market that we met the first major collector, Bob Lyons who showed us his marvelous collection. Not only did we get some of our first cast iron toys from him, but he also introduced us to Dale Kelley's *Antique Toy World* magazine.

Through the next three decades, toy shows became our main source for adding to our collection. Our first issue of *Toy World* contained an ad for an antique toy show to be held at the Rolling Meadows Holiday Inn near Chicago. And off we went.

Don Srenaski put on several shows at Rolling Meadows, with Dale Kelley eventually assuming the role of premier toy show promoter for what would became the foremost toy show in the United States—the St. Charles, Illinois, show. We bought more toys from the 74 shows we attended in St. Charles than from any other place.

We have made many good friends from going to toy shows. We met David Bausch in 1973 when we first attended his toy show in Macungie, Pennsylvania. Dave has been holding this show during the first week in August for more than thirty years. He is involved with what collectors consider one of the best antique toy shows in the country—the Allentown (PA) Antique Toy Show, held every November at the Allentown Fairgrounds.

Some other great shows that have contributed to our collection are John Carlisle's Toledo Toy Show, Phil Caponi's Philadelphia Toy Show, Bob Smith's Rochester Toy Show, and Larry Parker's Atlanta Toy Show.

Aside from the obvious source for finding new toys, shows also provide an opportunity to meet other collectors. Long-time friends and avid collectors John West, Dale Buchardt, Fred MacAdam, Ken Hutchinson, and Al Marwick were always helpful in identifying unusual toys and ready to discuss the hobby in general. I can remember the many times Bruce and Melinda Kling, Dick and Joan Ford, Don and Betty Jo Heim, and Tiny Moyer would talk over extended dinners about the finer points of collecting, and, back in 1976, when Bob Thurow held a get-together at his farm in Hampshire the evening before a St. Charles Toy Show.

Through the years we have visited the homes of many collectors. For us it was fun to stay at another collectors' house because you had more time to see their collections and learn how they acquired them. Many a time we stayed with Russ and Margarette Clifton on the way to St. Charles and sometimes went with them to antiques shops around Indiana. In New York, we always went to Grover Van Dexters' shop, Second Childhood, which has produced many treasures for us, and a visit to our old friend Jack Herbert was also a "must."

A trip to New England with a stay at Tony LaSala's resulted in a memorable trading session. And, in St. Louis, a visit to Jack and Kathy Stirnemann's was topped off with a night at the ballpark.

During our years in Michigan we made dozens of trips to see our old buddy Julian Thomas in Fenton. Julian, more than anyone else, has contributed to our knowledge of toys and to our collection. When a toy needed a driver or a tire or whatever, Julian had it. He and the Antique Toy Collectors of America were the first to reproduce old toy catalogs, which are essential in the identification and dating of toys. Lou Hertz's many books on toys as well as *Ernie Long's Dictionary of Toys*, *Lil Gottshalk's book on American Toy Cars and Trucks*, and *Al Aune's book on Arcade Toys*, to name just a few, have also been a great source of information for us. Rick Ralston's super book, *Cast Iron Floor Trains*, is a must for anyone thinking of collecting cast iron trains. Bob Saylor's knowledge of Kenton Toys and his collection of Kenton catalogs have been another source of historical data.

Through the years we have purchased pieces for our collection from dealers who specialize in pre-World War II automotive toys—Tom Sage, Bob Dalton, Jim Yeager, Jay Lowe, and Larry Bruch, to list just a few. I can remember buying some great iron automotive toys from Rich Garthoeffner, Dave Boyle, Perry Eichor, Gus Majeune, and Dave Smith back in the 1970s.

Auctions have also been a major source of toys for our collection. Thirty years ago Ted Maurer held some of the first toy auctions that we went to at the Lionville, Pennsylvania, firehall. Ted still holds many toy auctions each year. Some wonderful toys have come from Rick Opfer's auctions in Timonium, Maryland. For the past decade Bill Bertoia and Noel Barrett have held auctions that have had an awful lot of great stuff—if only I had more money! And now Randy Inman has been coming up with some super pieces, including a Flower Cycle.

I have yet to touch on a frequently unmentioned but very important part of collecting antique toys—the guys who repair them. Back in the dark ages of toy collecting if a cast iron toy had a crack or something missing it was either discarded or thrown in a drawer. The toys were more plentiful back then, and there were fewer collectors. Today it doesn't make any sense to ignore a nice old toy because it has a crack or is missing a wheel. Actually for years Russ Harrington has been fixing up cast iron toys and mechanical banks and making figures and parts for them. Some restorers like Ralph Lindenmoyer do wonderful work. Don Eckel (Salunga) makes wheels and figures and Arnie Prince also does cast iron repair.

Some unusual relationships have resulted from a mutual interest in old automotive toys. Years ago Tom Pasche, Larry Sieber, and I made some original cast iron vehicles. Tom and I made 125 J. L. Hudson vans and Larry made a line of limited edition trucks using the names Motorcade Toys. A few years later Rocky Romeo and I did a very limited edition of eight 1930 Lincoln coupes also in cast iron. Tom Sehloff in Oregon has for the past fifteen years made some wonderful cast iron cars and trucks, which are as nicely done as any made during the 1930s. Our good friend Jim Levengood builds lovely wood cabinets for our toys and receives cast iron toys in trade.

While the fun is in the search, as Al Marwick said, so much of the enjoyment of collecting also lies in the people you meet, the friends you make, and the interesting places you visit. Conventions held by the Antique Toy Collectors of America and the Mechanical Bank Collectors of America have taken us on trips throughout the United States and Europe. Some of those memories include enjoying a beer on the Orient Express, listening to an Umpah band while going from Stuttgart to Paris, watching a steeplechase while sipping wine

in Middleburg, Virginia, and stuffing ourselves with Cajun delicacies while wandering through Joe Daole and Patsy Powers' Atlanta Toy Museum. Visits to discuss toys such as our recent afternoon with Dick Dent, the grandson of the Dent Hardware Company's founder, who helped us with the history of Dent Hardware, have left us with memories just as wonderful and fond.

It's hard to imagine what our lives would have been like if we hadn't started collecting these toys. Our collection has enriched our lives, stimulated our imaginations, and consumed our days. Even today Stevie and I look forward to new toy shows, new toy auctions, and new opportunities to learn more about these toys.

So what's our advice to a novice collector?

Go out and find those old toys, enjoy the people you meet, and the places that collecting will take you. You will never regret it.

Bill and Stevie Weart
September 1999
Allentown

PART ONE: INTRODUCTION

1. The Industrial Revolution Creates a New Kind of Plaything

Since the 1980s, computers have forever changed the nature of playtime. Today children are as comfortable with a "computer mouse" as years ago their parents were with inserting C and D batteries in their toys. However, during the early part of the twentieth century, children were just discovering the luxuries of indulging their imaginations in creative playtime with a "store-bought toy."

The concept of children's play is a relatively new idea. Until the twentieth century, children's play was limited to quiet, after-church play. Privileged children had always been allowed to play with "Sunday toys" such as bisque dolls or delicate clock work mechanized tin toys. In fact, it is these "Sunday toys" that have survived today in such wonderful condition that we often see in museums and private collections. However, the majority of children never even saw these toys, but were content to play with their own home-made versions such as hand-carved toys or hand-sewn dolls.

With the advent of industrialization in the mid-nineteenth century, not only was there an industrial revolution, there was also a revolution in the lifestyles of the American family. And one of the biggest benefactors of this new industrialization was the American child who was no longer looked at just as an economic asset.

Until the twentieth century children of all classes had been expected to contribute to the economic survival of their families. Upperclass children were expected to make suitable marriages in order to add to or embellish family fortunes. City children became apprentices at an early age in trades and factories. Farm children worked along side their parents in the fields and barns.

By the turn of the century, parents began to enjoy the luxury of after-work socialization and had more time to help their children to develop social skills. They encouraged their children to learn to read, sing, and play a musical instrument. However, even into the turn of the century, there was a considerable debate about the value of letting children "play." American society still had a strong religious orientation, and many feared the consequences of frivolous play on their children's character. Many still believed that idle hands were devil's play and long hours of leisure could lead children into temptation and trouble. Educators, parents, and the clergy considered children "adults in waiting," and soon there was a national debate as to whether or not it was good to let children "play." To alleviate these feelings, most parents preferred playtime that focused on teaching skills that would profit children as adults. It was hoped that dolls would teach young girls to become better mothers, and that boys' toys would help them emulate their fathers' work.

During this same period small cast iron foundries were developing throughout the Northeastern states. Businessmen realized that these foundries could cast thousands of items necessary to make new products, and soon these foundries produced hardware for engines, sewing machines, bicycles, and ice boxes. Because some of these products were only seasonal in demand, many companies, faced with the prospect of having to lay off workers during the slack seasons, began to look for new products for their foundries to produce.

The idea of small cast iron toys for boys and girls represented an economic boon to the cast iron hardware industries. It provided an opportunity for these companies to maintain steady production and sales through the manufacture of miniature replicas for children. Before long, thousands of cast iron toys were being produced for the Christmas season and throughout the year.

Since the beginning of the twentieth century, the American male has had a love affair with the automobile and cast iron manufacturers saw an economic opportunity. Almost as quickly as the new automobiles rolled off the assembly lines, cast iron foundries were making toy models of the most popular automobiles, trucks, and farm equipment of the day. These toys had immediate appeal. They were colorful, detailed and realistic. Some had moveable parts, working accessories, removable drivers and passengers, and eventually electric headlights. City boys wanted to pretend to drive cars along busy city streets. They wanted trucks that dumped. They wanted fire engines, buses, and motorcycles. Farm boys wanted tractors, earthmovers, ditchers, and other farm and construction equipment.

At first only the upper classes bought these new toys for their children since most thrifty parents thought twice about spending their hard-earned money on toys. But gradually the cast iron toy companies began to produce a more diversified, tempting line of well-priced, affordable toys. Companies produced toys in five or six sizes ranging from 3 inches up to 15. The smaller toys sold in dime stores, while the larger toys sold for as much as one dollar in department stores.

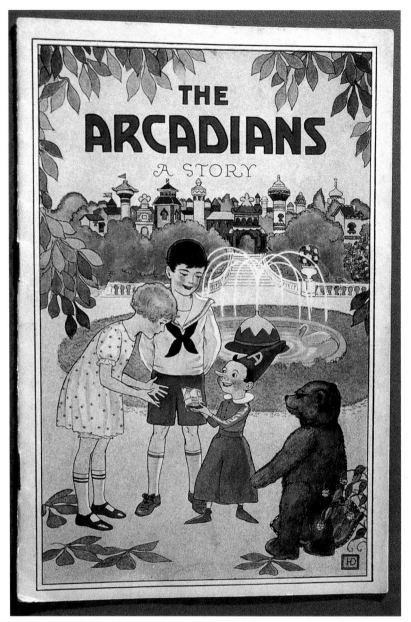

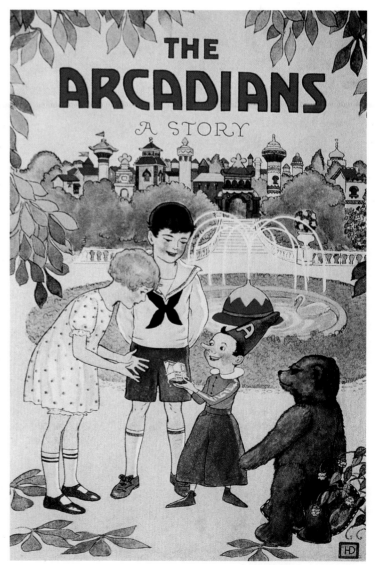

2. A Revolution in Toy Marketing

It is hard to believe that there was ever a time when toy buying was only a seasonal event. Today our society is inundated with advertising campaigns to encourage unbridled displays of hedonistic spending for children. Parents are bombarded with toy promotions and are shamed into going on toy-buying sprees all year-round through television, movies, media advertising and peer pressure. However, at the turn of the century, when the cast iron toy manufacturers began to advertise their new toys, toy buying was not part of most families' budgets, and these cast iron toy manufacturers instituted an advertising campaign that today looks almost naive and contrived. They stressed that their toys were teaching toys, durable, and made to last.

Toys That Teach

Understanding the concern parents had about the nature of play, manufacturers began to stress that their toys would help children to learn to be better, more productive adults. Penny banks encouraged thrift; miniature irons, ovens, stoves, and doll swings and carriages appealed to young girls' maternal and housekeeping skills; and boys wanted to enter the adult male world by pretending to drive cars and trucks that looked like those of their fathers.

Arcade Manufacturing Company, one of the largest cast iron toy manufacturers, advertised that the "famous Arcade Toys are approved by leading educators," and promised that all their toys had "educational value." "Wouldn't you like to play with these wonderful toys?" asked an Arcade catalog? "They are exactly like the real 'grown-up' thing . . . and made out of cast iron so they are hard to break." Hubley also stressed the educational value of their toys, advertising their toys as "Toys that Teach." "In response to the demands of both children and parents, an educational play feature is embodied in every Hubley Toy wherever possible. Modern parents are keen students of child psychology, and are coming more and more to insist upon toys that really work and do things."

Toys That Last

Catering to the thrifty nature of parents, companies also added another twist—durability. Cast iron toys were durable, built to last.

Arcade advertised their toys as "built solid, the Arcade Way of Construction Defying Destruction . . . it stands up under hard knocks"; "Toys that Last" boasted Grey Iron Casting Company; "Stop! Here are the toys you want. A whole box of indestructible toys," advertised Dent Hardware Company; "Beautiful colors . . . play features . . construction . . streamlining that is breath taking in its realism . . these features make every Hubley toy a sure winner of the hearts of the children and the dollars of the grown-ups . . . toys that are "Built to Stand the "Gaff of Play" (Hubley catalogs); and "prices are right . . . up to the minute design" (Kenton catalogs), promising every Kenton toy to be quality combined with low cost.

In fact most of the early toy catalogs emphasized their toys as "durable, solid and indestructible."

It is important to note despite these promises, many of the toys did not survive.

Toys That Children Love

Arcade advertised "cars, trucks, delivery vans that ran down hill without a string or a boy pulling it . . . toys as real as the real thing." (Many of these toys came with a pull cord.)

The companies exhorted children to play. Their advertising stressed the intricate nature of the toys and promised that the toys would "work."

Cast iron toy manufacturers created advertising campaigns that stressed the fact that children wished to be like their parents and the best way was to give them miniature versions of toys that were as "real as real could be."

The 1926 Arcade catalog promised that the "modern play sand piles demand an Auto Motor Dump Wagon to perform really efficient work for its youthful owners;" "with a Ford Weaver Wrecker, children's miniature toy accidents, instead of being a catastrophe, will be a source of amusement;" and "what boy will not follow excitedly after a clanging fire engine?"

The 1940 catalog told parents that "children that play with Arcade Toys today . . .[will] make the world of tomorrow."

Businesses soon understood the power of persuasive advertising slogans and the control a child's whim had on his parents' pocketbooks.

Colors That Delight The Eye

Cast iron toys were not only durable, well built, and ready for all kinds of play, but they were very colorful too. Because toy makers knew that color had visual appeal and was a great selling point, toys were painted and trimmed in vivid crimsons, greens, blues, yellows, and oranges, and then highlighted with contrasts of black and gold. Red became the most popular color and a best seller.

Dent stressed the word "attractive" to describe their toys . . . attractive toy, attractively decorated, highly attractively decorated . . attractively striped . . . a very attractive auto wrecking car . . . attractive colors . . . painted in bright colors.

Arcade noted that its toys had "bright colors, whirring blades and noise," and "that children and parents seem to like the noise."

Top: ARCADE MCCORMICK-DEERING THRESHER.
Bottom: ARCADE REO COUPE.

Top: The Reo was one of the most beautiful cars of the 1920s. Bottom: The Jaeger. The Kenton Jaeger Cement Mixer was not only one of the most common cast iron toys, it was one of the most beautiful and colorful. Toy companies found that red was the best selling color, but green, blue, and yellow were also popular.

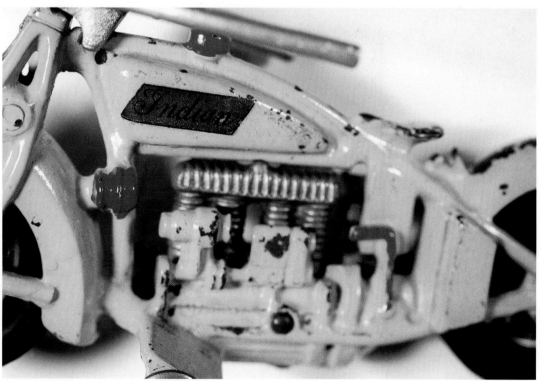

This is a beautifully detailed motorcycle.

Arcade did many special factory paint jobs and it was not unusual for Arcade to paint right over a finished toy if they had a rush order for a special paint treatment. Often taxi companies requested special paint jobs in their own colors for promotional toys or for some special occasion such as an annual employee Christmas party.

Special order Arcade cabs.

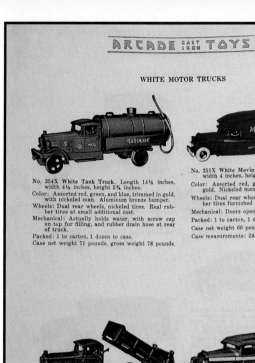

WHITE MOTOR TRUCKS

No. 254X White Tank Truck. Length 14⅛ inches, width 4½ inches, height 5¾ inches.

Color: Assorted red, green, and blue, trimmed in gold, with nickeled man. Aluminum bronze bumper.

Wheels: Dual rear wheels, nickeled tires. Real rubber tires at small additional cost.

Mechanical: Actually holds water, with screw cap on top for filling, and rubber drain hose at rear of truck.

Packed: 1 to carton, 1 dozen to case.

Case net weight 71 pounds, gross weight 78 pounds.

No. 251X White Moving Van. Length 13⅜ inches, width 4 inches, height 4¾ inches.

Color: Assorted red, green, and blue, trimmed in gold. Nickeled man and bumper.

Wheels: Dual rear wheels, nickeled tires. Real rubber tires furnished at small additional cost.

Mechanical: Doors open in rear.

Packed: 1 to carton, 1 dozen to case.

Case net weight 66 pounds, gross weight 82 pounds.

Case measurements: 24x14x14¾ inches.

No. 258X White Dump Truck. Length 13¼ inches, width 4½ inches, height 6¾ inches raised, 4½ inches lowered.

Color: Assorted red, green, and blue. Trimmed in aluminum bronze and gold. Nickeled man.

Wheels: Dual rear wheels, nickeled tires. Real rubber tires at small additional cost.

Mechanical: Dump body raised by releasing catch and end gate opens.

Packed: 1 to carton, 1 dozen to case.

Case net weight 62 pounds, gross weight 70 pounds.

No. 319X White Bus. Length 13¼ inches, width 3½ inches, height 3¾ inches.

Color: Assorted red, green, and blue. Nickeled driver and tires.

Wheels: Dual rear wheels and nickeled tires. Rubber tires at small additional cost.

Packed: 1 to carton, 1 dozen to case.

Case net weight 48 pounds, gross weight 60 pounds.

Case measurements: 25¼x14¼x8¼ inches.

ARCADE MFG. CO. FREEPORT, ILL.

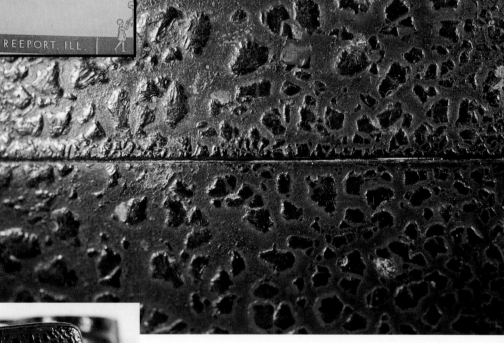

Paint condition on these toys can vary. The paint on some Kenton toys never completely cured resulting in a condition that collectors call "alligatoring" or "floating islands of paint." However, this condition does not necessarily affect the value, because many collectors are thrilled to get a car with its original paint.

Kenton had a paint problem with some of their toys. It is not unusual for Kenton paint to mottle or craze over time. We surmise that it might have been because the correct amount of dryer was not always used in their paint compound, which meant the paint never completely dried. Dent was also known to have paint curing problems.

Kenton toys, which some believe have been repainted because their axles are painted, may actually be original factory finishes. Kenton at times dipped their toys with the wheels in place, and then decorated them as opposed to the more common practice of decorating the wheels and then installing them.

Kilgore used an opalescent finish in an array of charming color combinations—"beautiful pearly greens, reds, blues, etc. reflecting light rays as a shimmering opal."

Size Was Another Marketing Tool

Toys were made in many sizes.

Today many collectors collect by size and often seek complete series of all the sizes of a particular toy. It is interesting to note that generally the largest sizes are the most difficult to find because they were the most expensive and fewer were sold especially during the Depression years.

The lengths of the toys pictured in this book are the actual measured lengths to the nearest 1/4 inch. In some cases, the lengths may actually differ from the stated lengths listed in the manufacturers' catalogs. This is because it was not un-common for companies to exaggerate the actual lengths of a toy by as much as 1/2 inch. We surmise that this discrepancy was an attempt to gain a sales advantage over competitors since buyers often bought toys by size (size often being the greatest determinant for price). For example, in 1932, a 3-inch cast iron toy was about nineteen cents at the five and dime store, while a 6-inch toy usually sold for fifty to seventy-five cents in a toy or department store.

Toys That Look Real

Another selling point was detail and accuracy. Children wanted miniature replicas like the 'real thing.'

Arcade more than any other manufacturer made a line of replicas of current production vehicles and Hubley frequently got the rights to produce accurate replicas of well-known brand names. Some of the best known of Hubley's "exclusive right toys" were miniatures of Borden's trucks, Indian and Harley-Davidson motorcycles, Packard cars, Huber road roll-ers, Bell Telephone trucks, General Electric, and Maytag appliances. Because of these exacting details, the company gained a reputation for making toys that were usually more complex than those of other cast iron toy makers.

From the beginning manufacturers realized that if they were going to promote real life toys, the toys would have to operate like the real ones. Gradually the companies experimented with more working parts. Children loved toys with moveable parts and toy makers realized that these working parts were an essential part of their ability to compete for their youthful market.

Arcade Weaver wrecker.

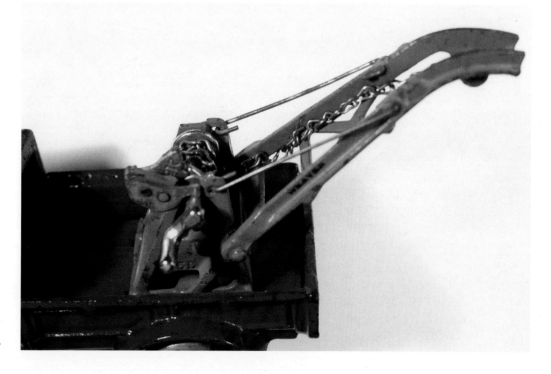

Detail of a Weaver boom.

Detail of a hose reel in the Arcade Mack Chemical truck.

Detail of an Arcade Mack Dump Truck lift mechanism.

This shows the Hubley Packard straight eight engine.

Realistic front grill with hood ornament—Kilgore Graham.

For a few years, cars such as this Hubley Chrysler Airflow came equipped with electric headlights.

Detail of a Hubley Ahrens-Fox piston pump.

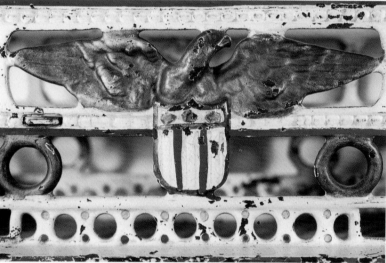

Collectors like cast iron vehicles because they are so well made and have charming details such as this eagle insignia on the Hubley fire engine.

Seated passengers from a bus. Note that they hook onto the bus seat.

And little figures to drive and travel in the vehicles. Note the charming detail of this seated passenger's scarf.

A Hubley cast iron mailman.

An Arcade policeman cast iron bank. The banks, unlike the cars, which were riveted together, were always screwed together so that you could take the money out.

3. The Manufacture of Cast Iron Toys

The cast iron industry came about through ingenuity and imagination. Most of the leading factories built their fortunes through their ability to keep up with popular tastes, manufacturing hardware for iceboxes, locks, sewing machines, and bicycles. Their production processes enabled them to cast thousands of components cheaply, quickly, and efficiently, and nowhere did these methods work better than in the manufacture of cast iron toys.

While the production of these toys was an elaborate step by step process, it required limited skills and expertise beyond those of the pattern maker. The pattern maker had to make the brass patterns for a toy based on the sketches of the full-size vehicle. Often working from blue prints, he added the detail and realism that became important selling points.

The toy parts were first cast in sand molds. The liquid iron was poured into these molds, allowed to cool, and then the mold was pulled apart. Often some of the sand remained glued to the new iron surface so the parts had to be placed in large tumblers. Tumbling stars helped loosen the sand particles out of the crevices of the toy parts. Next the parts were riveted together. Sanding belts were used to polish the roofs and hoods of the toys.

Painting the toys was also an intricate process. First the toys were submerged into vats of enamel paint, then hung over drip pans to dry. Usually the company hired young ladies to hand paint and stripe the details on each car. They would paint on details such as headlights, tires, fenders, and, in some cases, drivers. (Kenton assembled their smaller toys complete with axles and wheels, dipped them into the vat of paint to give them the main color coat, and then hand painted the tires, headlights, fenders, roofs, and stripes in silver or gold.) Occasionally newly painted toys brushed against each other, resulting in smudges of other colors on some toys. Finally, the toys would be packed into cartons, usually by the dozen. Often the companies would store the toys in advance of the busy Christmas season.

We do not know when the first toy Model T's were manufactured, but we do know that they were produced early in the twentieth century, probably dating from the late teens; obviously production was limited during the war years. We have not been able to find many catalogs from the pre-World War I era.

Today many collectors store those toys with rubber tires on wooden blocks to prevent the old rubber from getting flat spots.

There was a tremendous variety in the various wheels and tires used on these vehicles. Manufacturers produced painted wheels, nickel plated wheels, wooden hubs, white rubber tires, black rubber tires, and other variations of tires and wheels.

ARCADE CAST IRON TOYS

"THEY LOOK REAL"

ARCADE CAST IRON TOYS are patterned carefully and accurately to duplicate in miniature the models they represent. They are made of a high grade grey iron. Enamels and lacquers used in their finish are made especially for our own use. In addition to Cast Iron Toys, refer to pages 30 and 31 for Popular Games, and to pages 28 and 29 for Garages and Gas Filling Station, made of wood.

RUBBER WHEELS

These are actual size illustrations of the real rubber disc wheels used on all ARCADE toy pleasure automobiles, trucks, trailers, racers and airplanes. The centers are colored as illustrated. They not only enhance the appearance of the toys and add to their realism, but protect polished floor surfaces.

A nickel plated spoke wheel from a Hubley Crash Car Motorcycle.

A painted spoke wheel from a transitional Hubley Ladder Truck.

A decorative painted spoked road roller wheel from a Hubley Huber Road Roller.

A Hubley black rubber tire with a nickel plated steel spoke wheel.

An Arcade white rubber tractor tire with a painted center.

The rear roller wheel.

Left:
A Hubley rubber tire with a wooden hub.

An Arcade Model T painted spoke wheel.

An Arcade white rubber tire with a cast iron spoked wheel.

An Arcade Model T nickel plated spoke wheel.

An Arcade taxicab painted disc wheel.

An Arcade cast iron disc wheel with a painted nickel plated center.

4. The End of the Cast Iron Toy Industry

The two World Wars interfered with cast iron toy manufacture. Patriotism required that companies devote themselves to the war effort and the raw materials were important to producing war machinery and tools.

After World War II, most companies making cast iron toys did not return to their pre-war activity. Higher labor costs and competition from the die cast and plastic toy industry made post-war cast iron toy production too expensive. One of the few exceptions was the Kenton Company, which managed to manufacture cast iron toys through 1953, while Hubley produced cast iron Bell Telephone trucks into the late 1940s.

And thus ended what had been a unique and almost exclusively American industry.

Twentieth-Century Changes in Parental Attitudes about Giving Toys

It is interesting to note the changes in parental attitudes towards giving children toys. Richard Dent, whose grandfather Henry founded the Dent Hardware Company, remembers that when he was growing up in the 1930s his father (who was then the president of the company) only brought home toys for Christmas, and occasionally cast iron cannons for the Fourth of July.

Dent also fondly remembers one day in the 1920s when he was in the first grade. His father came to school dressed like Santa Claus and gave each member of the class a Dent toy.

By the 1950s, toy buying was still mostly promoted during the Christmas season. Children had to work hard to convince their parents to give them toys at other times of the year. And it was not unusual for children to earn extra pocket money for toys by doing errands, mowing lawns, shoveling snow, or washing family cars.

5. Identifying A Toy

Since some of the toys listed in this book have no manufacturers' markings and no catalog attributions, we have made educated guesses as to the maker.

Identifying makers becomes an acquired skill. And it is important to study catalogs to help get a feel for the company's products.

Arcade toys are some of the most avidly collected cast iron toys because, unlike many of the other cast iron toys, they are easier to identify since most of them are marked. Not only did Arcade put its name inside the toy in raised letters, but they frequently used decals. Often the company also marked its tires.

It is interesting to note that while Arcade, Vindex, and Champion marked practically all their toys, many manufacturers did not mark their toys at all. Hubley only marked a small percentage of their toys, and along with Arcade and Vindex often used decals to identify the manufacturers. Kenton marked some of their toys beginning in the mid-1930s, and Freidag and Kilgore marked their toys only occasionally. Others such as Dent, A. C. Williams, and Globe never marked their toys at all. Champion put its name on the outside of its toys, while North and Judd marked their toys on the inside.

Left:
Close-up of an Arcade decal. Arcade was one of the few companies to mark almost all their toys. In the late 1920s the company started to use decals. We do not know why the company used decals on some toys and not on others.

Vindex also used decals on their toys.

Detail of a Hubley decal. Hubley was another company that marked their toys.

North and Judd marked their toys with raised letters. This is an Austin-Bantam Roadster.

6. A Value Guide

In order to help the reader determine the relative desirability of each toy shown in this book, we have included the following value guide. At the end of each caption a letter appears ranging from A to K to indicate value. The category into which each toy is placed is based on a toy's expected retail price if in excellent condition, all original and complete, with 90% of the original paint. For example, if a toy in excellent condition could be expected to retail between $900-1100, it would be assigned to the E category.

It is important to understand that the value of a toy is not only dependent upon its scarcity and general aesthetic appeal, both of which affect its desirability, but also on its condition. A toy with 90% of its original paint and in overall excellent condition would bring about $1000; however, if in poor condition, it might bring only $200. And considerably more than $1000, if in mint condition.

Developing an "eye" is part of the collecting process. Experienced collectors understand that pricing is determined as much by condition as by rarity and aesthetic appeal. It is always wise to buy a toy in the best condition available and trade up whenever possible.

And perhaps, toy collector Malcolm Forbes (1919-1990) summed it up best with this statement: "Buy only what you like. Measure a work by the joy and satisfaction it will bring. And if you want to collect as an investment, become a dealer."

Value Categories

A	$25-100
B	$100-200
C	$200-400
D	$400-700
E	$700-1100
F	$1100-1700
G	$1700-2500
H	$2500-4000
I	$4000-6000
J	$6000-10,000
K	$10,000+

Neither the authors nor the publisher are responsible for any outcomes that may result from using this price guide.

Some of the most common abbreviations used to describe cast iron toys are:

CI = Cast iron
NP = Nickel plated

R = Equipped with rubber tires.
E = Electrical toys

For greater clarity we have used only one symbol in this book, an asterisk (*) appears to indicate toys for which we were not able to locate a catalog number.

PART TWO: THE CAST IRON TOY MANUFACTURERS

1. ARCADE "They look real"

The Arcade Manufacturing Company incorporated in 1885 in Freeport, Illinois. Its president was L.L. Munn; its Secretary, his son, L.L. Munn; Jr. Charles Morgan was Vice President; and E.H. Morgan was the treasurer and general manager. The first Arcade factory was built in February of 1893. From the beginning the company manufactured light hardware, house finishings, specialties, and wood and iron toys. Its 1902 catalog advertised doll carriages, doll swings, girls' toys such as play irons and ovens, banks, toy iron trains, and "Busy Boy" toys. In 1908 the company introduced its first miniature horse-drawn toy, the Panama Dump Wagon. The flyer advertised that the "1908 model has a new combination of colors that shouts at the passerby. The rest of the toy is just as good as ever."

In 1921 Arcade made an alliance with the Yellow Cab company, and in 1922 they began to manufacture a miniature replica of the well-known cab. Eventually other toy companies would follow its example and begin to reproduce miniatures of well-known brand name items.

Details of some of the many special promotion Arcade taxi-cabs. Arcade often produced these cabs for specific events.

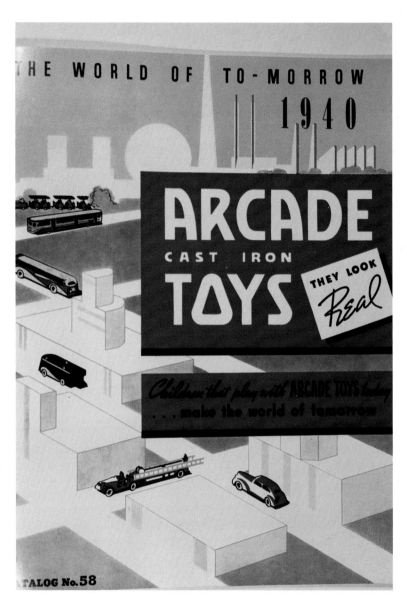

Our Factory at Freeport, Illinois

AUTOMOBILES

*TOY COUPE, 9", 1922-1927. The Arcade catalog says that the "Toy Coupe" is built in the same unbreakable way as the Toy Yellow Cab. It has a separate driver and spare tire (with 1922 in raised numbers). This version has spoked wheels. G

*TOY COUPE, 9", 1922-1927. This toy differs from the yellow and black toy shown separately because it has disc rather than spoked wheels and probably was made near the end of the production run. F

Close-up of Andy Gump's face.

142-1 ANDY GUMP and OLD 348, 7 1/4", 1923-1931. This is the deluxe version. H

ANDY GUMP CAR from the 1926 Arcade catalog.

ARCADE IRON TOYS

ANDY GUMP AND OLD 348

Licensed by the Sidney Smith Corporation

No. 1 Andy Gump has a red tie, white shirt, blue suit, and brown sport hat with green hat-band. Old 348 has a bright red body with green trimmings, green disc wheels with red hub caps, white tires, and aluminum license plates. Size: Length over all 7¼ inches, wheel base 4⅞ inches, height 6 inches, width 4 inches.

No. 2 Andy Gump: Car, red; Andy and Wheels, full nickel plated; without license plate or front crank. Size, weight, packing: same as No. 1.

No. 3 Andy Gump: Car is red (only), wheels nickel plated with green disc and no license plate nor front crank. Andy is painted green with white collar and flesh colored face. Size, weight, packing: same as No. 1.

PACKED:
Each in a decorated paper carton, 12 in a case. Case net weight 36 pounds, gross 45 pounds. Case dimensions 19x12¼x8¼ inches.

ARCADE MFG. CO. FREEPORT, ILL.

142-2 ANDY GUMP and OLD 348, 7 1/4",
1926-1930, also 1933. This is the medium-priced version. The toy pictured is stamped on both sides "A Century of Progress-Chicago 1933." We are not aware of any others with this identification. The Andy Gump Car is not pictured in catalogs after this year, so Arcade must have made a special run of them just to sell at the Fair. G.

142-3 ANDY GUMP and OLD 348, 7 1/4",
1926-1930. This is the economy model. F

*CHEVROLET UTILITY COUPE, 6 3/4", 1925-1928. Came with a nickel plated driver and a separate spare tire. E

*CHEVROLET SUPERIOR SEDAN, 6 3/4", 1925-1928. Came with a nickel plated driver and a separate spare tire. E

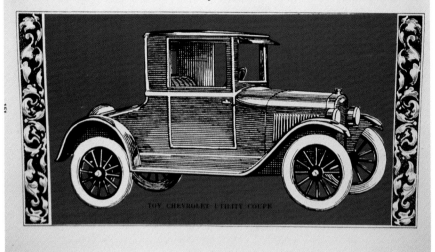

Entire Chevrolet Line Perfectly Reduced to Pocked-sized Models

TOY CHEVROLET UTILITY COUPE

A CHEVROLOT COUPE from the 1926 Arcade catalog.

*CHEVROLET SUPERIOR ROADSTER, 6 3/4", 1925-1928. Came with a nickel plated driver and a separate spare tire. E

*CHEVROLET SUPERIOR TOURING CAR, 6 3/4", 1925-1928. Came with a nickel plated driver and a separate spare tire. E

121 IMPROVED CHEVROLET COUPE, 8", 1926-1928. This toy did not come with a driver and has a separate nickel plated spare tire, which in some cases has a round paper disk attached with a dealer's logo. F

122 IMPROVED CHEVROLET SEDAN, 8", 1926-1928. Like the 8" Chevrolet Coupe, this Sedan came with a nickel plated spare tire and no driver. H

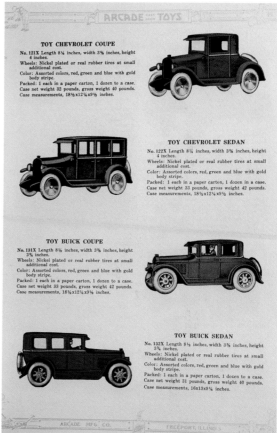

ARCADE CAST IRON TOYS

TOY CHEVROLET COUPE
No. 121X Length 8¼ inches, width 3⅝ inches, height 4 inches.
Wheels: Nickel plated or real rubber tires at small additional cost.
Color: Assorted colors, red, green and blue with gold body stripe.
Packed: 1 each in a paper carton, 1 dozen to a case.
Case net weight 32 pounds, gross weight 40 pounds.
Case measurements, 18½x12¼x9½ inches.

TOY CHEVROLET SEDAN
No. 122X Length 8¼ inches, width 3⅝ inches, height 4 inches.
Wheels: Nickel plated or real rubber tires at small additional cost.
Color: Assorted colors, red, green and blue with gold body stripe.
Packed: 1 each in a paper carton, 1 dozen to a case.
Case net weight 33 pounds, gross weight 42 pounds.
Case measurements, 18½x12¼x9½ inches.

TOY BUICK COUPE
No. 131X Length 8½ inches, width 3⅝ inches, height 3⅞ inches.
Wheels: Nickel plated or real rubber tires at small additional cost.
Color: Assorted colors, red, green and blue with gold body stripe.
Packed: 1 each in a paper carton, 1 dozen to a case.
Case net weight 33 pounds, gross weight 42 pounds.
Case measurements, 18½x12¼x9½ inches.

TOY BUICK SEDAN
No. 132X Length 8½ inches, width 3⅝ inches, height 3⅞ inches.
Wheels: Nickel plated or real rubber tires at small additional cost.
Color: Assorted colors, red, green and blue with gold body stripe.
Packed: 1 each in a paper carton, 1 dozen to a case.
Case net weight 31 pounds, gross weight 40 pounds.
Case measurements, 16x13x9¼ inches.

ARCADE MFG. CO.   FREEPORT, ILLINOIS.

In 1929 Arcade stopped painting their 8" Chevrolet Coupe and Sedan and their Buick Coupe and Sedan tutone and offered them in a solid color. This no doubt reduced the cost of painting these toys.

121 CHEVROLET COUPE, 8", 1929. In 1929 this 8" Coupe replaced the gray/black version. It was available in assorted colors apparently for only one year, which makes this toy very scarce. H

*FORD COUPE, 6 1/2", 1925. This, the earliest of the Model T Coupes made by Arcade, is known as the tulip body version because of the sweeping curve of the body below the belt line resembling the shape of the flower. This toy came with a separate nickel plated driver. D

Page from Arcade catalog showing a Toy Ford Coupe.

*FORD COUPE, 6 1/2", 1926-1927. This body design is the second Model T Coupe that Arcade made, and like all the other Arcade 6" Model T Fords, it came with a nickel plated driver. D

103 FORD TUDOR SEDAN, 6 1/2", 1926-1927. Came with a nickel plated driver. E

For a period of time Arcade offered their Model T Fords and Chevrolets with the option of rubber tires, for a slight additional cost. Most were sold with the standard all cast iron wheels. Those that were sold with rubber tires are usually found today with their tires either in very poor condition or completely missing. A Model T or Chevrolet with good original tires is very desirable.

*FORD TOURING CAR, 6 1/2", 1923-1927. Came with a nickel plated driver. D

*FORD TUDOR (CENTER DOOR) SEDAN, 6 1/2", 1923-1927. Came with a nickel plated driver. D

*FORD FORDOR SEDAN, 6 1/2", 1923-1927. Came with a nickel plated driver. D

103 FORD TUDOR SEDAN, 6 1/2", 1927. This toy, available in four colors, came with nickel plated wheels and driver and replaced the earlier all black version. E

*FORD FORDOR SEDAN, 6 1/2", 1927. This toy replaced the earlier all black Sedan. It came with nickel plated wheels and driver. E

*FORD COUPE, 6 3/4", 1927. This was the last of the three Arcade Model T Coupes to be introduced and it was only made for a year. It came in four colors and had a nickel plated driver and nickel plated wheels. E

*FORD COUPE, 5", 1923-1926. This was the first of two 5" Model T Coupes that Arcade produced and it came with nickel plated wheels. C

*FORD COUPE, 5", 1927. Arcade brought out this 5" Coupe to replace the earlier, more boxy-shaped version. It was only made for one year and came with nickel plated wheels. D

*FORD FORDOR SEDAN, 5", 1923-1927. This Model T always came with nickel plated wheels and no driver. C

106 FORD COUPE, 6 1/2", 1928-1932. Arcade produced the 6" Ford Model A Coupe with a rumble seat and nickel plated driver and wheels. Rubber tires were an extra cost option. E

108 FORD TUDOR SEDAN, 6 1/2", 1928-1932. This Model A came with nickel plated wheels and driver and is difficult to find, especially in nice condition. G

107 FORD FORDOR SEDAN, 6 1/2",
1928-1932. This Model A came with
nickel plated wheels and driver. F

123 FORD FIRE CHIEF'S COUPE, 6 1/2", 1932-1933.
This Model A Ford Coupe is very scarce. It doesn' t
have a rumble seat. It came with a nickel plated driver
and rubber tired, nickel plated wheels. H

118 FORD TUDOR SEDAN, 5",
1928-1933. This was the only style of
a Model A Ford Sedan that Arcade
made in the 5" size. These toys came
without drivers and with nickel plated
wheels. C

116 FORD COUPE, 5", 1928-1932.
This Model A Ford Coupe doesn't have
a rumble seat. It only came with nickel
plated wheels and without a driver. D

116 FORD COUPE, 5", 1928-1932. This toy is the more common of the Arcade 5" Model A Ford Coupes. It has a rumble seat, no driver, and nickel plated wheels. C

147 REO COUPE, 9", 1931-1933. The REO is one of Arcade's most attractive toys. It has an opening rumble seat, a nickel plated grill, a nickel plated driver (attached to the toy by a screw), and two sidemount spare tires. It came in two color combinations. H

147 REO COUPE, 9", 1931-1933. The two-tone gray version of the REO is the hardest to find. This one has optional rubber tires. I

Right: Detail of a closed rumble seat.

Detail of an open rumble seat.

132 BUICK SEDAN, 8 1/2", 1926-1928. This toy has the paint scheme that Arcade used for the first years that it made the Buick. H

132 BUICK SEDAN, 8 1/2", 1926-1928. This appears to have been a special factory paint job. Underneath the toy a chip-free coat of Arcade Buick green appears. It was not unusual for Arcade to paint right over a finished toy if they had an order for a special paint treatment. This was usually done for taxi companies who may have wanted to order toys in their own colors for some special occasion. H

131 BUICK COUPE, 8 1/2", 1926-1928. The Arcade Buicks are fairly difficult to find. They came with a separate spare tire and a nickel plated driver. H

131 BUICK COUPE, 8 1/2", 1929-1930. In the year 1929, Arcade painted their Buicks in assorted colors. They came with nickel plated wheels, a spare tire, and driver. H

109 COUPE, 5 3/4", 1932-1933. This rather scarce toy is not marked "Arcade," which was very unusual because most Arcade toys were marked. D

125 DESOTO SEDAN, 6 1/4",1936.
Came with a nickel plated grill. D

146 DESOTO SEDAN, 4", 1936.
Came with a nickel plated grill. B

FORD SEDAN and COVERED WAGON, 1938-1939. This is a very well done reproduction of the Arcade 197 set of car and trailer. They were made in aluminum by Jim Malone in an edition of around 50 in about 1975. B

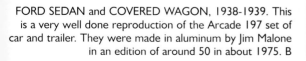

Arcade introduced their first Mullins Red Cap luggage trailer in 1937. It sold as a set with a two-door sedan for twenty-five cents. Trailers were first coming into fashion in the 1930s when motoring and camping was becoming an American leisure time activity. These small luggage trailers offered an opportunity to bring along more luggage and equipment. For many years the Mullins Company, which was founded in 1872, fabricated metal ornaments and cornices for buildings. But, in 1882, Mr. Mullins bought the company and by 1919 the company was making automotive stampings for REO, Franklin, Locomobile, Pierce-Arrow, and Cadillac. In the 1920s, the automotive business declined and Mullins began to make tubs for washing machines. The company produced its first Mullins Red Cap in 1936. In 1974, the company closed its doors forever.

*FORD SEDAN and MULLINS RED CAP TRAILER, 1937-1941. The 1938 Arcade catalog shows the Red Cap Trailer with another sedan but the toys pictured were obtained together out of an attic. Perhaps they were sold together or got hitched up at a later date by their young owner. F

*MULLINS RED CAP TRAILER, 3 1/4", 1937-1941. This was only available with a two door Sedan. B

TAXICABS

Arcade made their earlier taxis in three sizes, 9 inch, 8 inch, and 5 1/4 inch, and painted them in a variety of color schemes. They even made ones with phone numbers and company names on their doors and roofs. Some of their standard taxis, as well as some special orders, are shown.

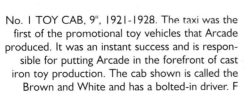

No. 1 TOY CAB, 9", 1921-1928. The taxi was the first of the promotional toy vehicles that Arcade produced. It was an instant success and is responsible for putting Arcade in the forefront of cast iron toy production. The cab shown is called the Brown and White and has a bolted-in driver. F

Arcade did many special factory paint jobs and it was not unusual for Arcade to paint right over a finished toy if they had a rush order for a special paint treatment. Often taxi companies requested special paint jobs for promotional toys in their own colors to be used for some special occasion.

No. 1 TOY CAB, 9", 1921-1928. Special order. G

An ARCADE 1925 catalog page showing the toy taxis that had made Arcade a major force in the toy industry in the 1920s.

The 1925 Arcade catalog noted, "This is the famous Toy Yellow Cab which has taken the country by storm. New and novel, its appeal to children is strong and direct; kiddies prefer it to all other toys . . . Each cab is sturdily made from grey iron and is practically unbreakable; it has no clock work to get out of order. Each has a removable driver fastened firmly in place with a bolt and nut." (Freidag and Hubley also were successful with their Yellow Cabs.)

"We also furnish cabs in other popular finishes. The most attractive of these are Brown and White, Black and White, and Red Top cabs." Arcade also produced a Yellow Cab Bank.

No. 1 TOY CAB, 9", 1921-1928. Special order Yellow Cab—Arlington. G

No. 1 TOY CAB, 9", 1921-1928. This cab is unusual because it never had any Yellow Cab markings stamped on its doors. F

*CAB BANK, 8", 1923-1926. Came with a bolted-in driver and a removable steel coin trap—"could hold many coins." E

*TOY CAB BANK, 8", 1923-1926. Has the name "City Cab" painted on the rear doors. The roof has the words "We use Betholine" painted on the roof. The roof is dark blue and the hood and fenders are black. G

*TOY CAB BANK, 8", 1923-1926.
Came with a bolted-in driver and steel
coin trap. E

*TOY CAB BANK, 8", 1927-1928. Came with a
bolted-in driver and steel coin trap. This version
has a stripe that runs along the side of the hood and
is scarcer than the earlier version. F

No. 2 TOY CAB, 8", 1923-1926. This special order
taxi has the telephone number ATL 4000 on its
roof and Red Top Cab Co. on the doors. G

No. 2 TOY CAB, 8", 1923-1926.
This toy is equipped with rubber
tires and a bolted-in driver. E

No. 2 TOY CAB 8", 1923-1926. This is
the Checker Cab version and has the
bolted-in driver and rubber tires. F

No. 2 TOY CAB, 8", 1927-1928. Has a
bolted-in driver and rubber tires. E

No. 3 TOY CAB, 5 1/4", 1926-1930. This small 5 1/4" taxi is the most difficult of the three sizes to find. It has a separate spare tire held on with a cotter pin. In 1929 it was made with a stripe along the hood and had a 153 catalog number. E

155 LIMOUSINE YELLOW CAB, 8 1/4", 1927-1932. This taxi is actually a copy of the real Mile Merchant Taxi produced by the Yellow Cab Co. It is known as the flat top cab by collectors. It came with two nickel plated cowl lamps, a nickel plated driver, a spare tire, and a separate screwed-on rear license plate. H

1620 FORD TAXI, 6 3/4", 1933-1934. Almost all these taxis were sold at the Century of Progress World's Fair in 1933-34 and they have that designation on the roof. The toy has a nickel plated grill. This car was also sold as a Ford Sedan 1620 in assorted colors. F

1570 CHECKER CAB, 9", 1932-1933. The toy pictured is a fine reproduction of the original Arcade taxi. An original Arcade taxi is very scarce and extremely desirable. It was only made for a couple of years. Toy pictured. D

1580 YELLOW CAB, 8 1/4", 1936-1937. This taxi is known as the Parmalee Cab and has a nickel plated grill and rear license plate. It is considered quite scarce and desirable. H

1590 YELLOW CAB, 8 1/4", 1940-1941. The body of this cab is a single piece casting. The driver and passenger casting is riveted in. D

RACERS

175 AUSTIN RACER, 3/4", 1932-1936. B

139 BULLET RACER, 7 5/8", 1931-1932. This is a scarce toy. It has separate nickeled exhausts, driver, and mechanic. It came with nickeled plated disc wheels or spoked wheels with rubber tires. F

307 FAGEOL SAFETY COACH, 12", 1925-1931. In 1925 this toy came only in ivory, but in later years it was produced in green, blue, ivory, or red. The toy came with a nickel plated driver and is fairly easy to find. D

319 WHITE BUS, 13 1/4", 1929-1932. This bus came with dual rear wheels, a nickel plated driver and dual side mounts. In 1929 it only came in blue. In 1930 the dual sidemounts were discontinued and it was available in three colors. H

313 YELLOW PARLOR COACH, 13 1/4", 1926-1930. This large bus came with dual sidemounts and a nickel plated driver. It has dual rear wheels. H

309 A.C.F. COACH, 11 1/2", 1927-1930. The unique feature of this bus is its opening front door. It has dual rear wheels and a nickel plated driver. H

316 DOUBLE DECK YELLOW COACH, 8", 1929-1939. Came with a nickel plated driver. E

315 DOUBLE DECKER YELLOW COACH, 13 1/2", 1925-31. This bus came in red, green, or blue and had a nickel plated driver and dual rear wheels. The seats on the upper deck are made of steel. G

40 DOUBLE DECKER YELLOW COACH, 13 1/2", 1925-1927. This is the same bus as the 315 but only came in brown with "Fifth Avenue Buss." on the side instead of "Yellow Coach." These are difficult to find. G

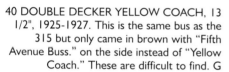

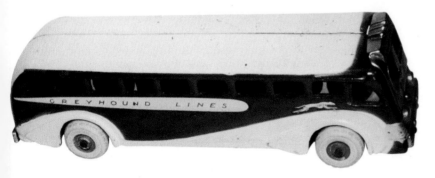

4380 GREYHOUND BUS, 9", 1938-1941. This toy has separate nickel plated front and rear pieces that are held in place by the two body halves. C

3850 GMC BUS, 7 3/4", 1936-1941. This toy came in several colors and with several logos on the roof. This toy has "Coast to Coast-GMC" on the roof. C

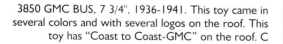

3180 DOUBLE DECKER BUS, 7 3/4", 1940-1941. Arcade's last double deck bus has a nickel plated grill and came with three nickel plated passengers. D

By 1922 toys represented five percent of the Arcade factory output. With the production of its first dollar toy, Arcade began to realize that there was a profit in larger toys. Their advertising boasted their toys as "the cleverest reproduction of something everybody knows you ever saw." Children wanted to buy the familiar things they saw on the street. And just as girls were urging their parents to buy baby-like dolls so boys wanted cars and trucks that looked like the real thing:

"The latest addition to the Arcade Line of Iron Toys is so realistic that it seems to have rolled right off Fifth Avenue . . . Children like the 'true to life' appearance that children appreciate so quickly. Built solid, the Arcade Way of Construction Defying Destruction . . . it stands up under hard knocks." "Real playthings out of their everyday world."

Arcade not only courted city kids, but being an Illinois-based company they realized that America was still largely an agrarian society. In 1923, the company manufactured its first toy Fordson Tractor. Like the city cars, these farm vehicles were also painted in the bright colors that children liked—crimson reds, greens, and gold trims. Soon Arcade was offering extras such as optional rubber tires on their toys.

During the late 1920s, Arcade started to use "decals." However, we do not know why the company used them on some of their toys and not on others.

During the dark years of the Depression when toy sales severely dropped, the Greyhound Trailer Bus, made from 1933-1936, probably saved Arcade from bankruptcy. In 1932, Arcade made a deal with General Motors, the Chicago World's Fair Planning Commission and Greyhound Bus Company, to produce a miniature toy replica of the Century of Progress Trailer Bus. These buses, made by GM, carried passengers around the vast fairgrounds of the Century of Progress fair by the Chicago lake front. Arcade was able to sell their buses by the thousands at the fair, which lasted from 1933-1934, and offered the two largest sizes in their catalogs until 1936. Because of the huge number of buses made during these years, they are considered easy to obtain today.

With the approach of World War II, Arcade was forced to cease production, and, by 1943, the company ceased its toy line forever.

GREYHOUND TRAILER BUS, five sizes,
1933-1936. The catalog lists them as 3250,
14 1/2", E; 3210, 12", D; 3220, 10 1/2", C;
3230, 7 1/2", *5 3/4", C

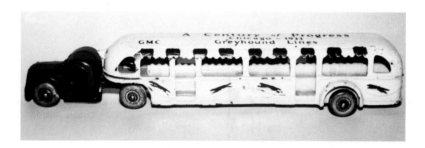

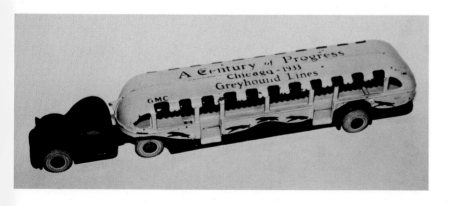

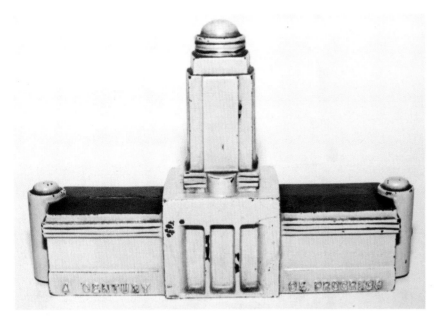

869 "A CENTURY OF PROGRESS" BANK 7", 1933-1934. A miniature of a modernistic building at the Chicago World's Fair. F

4360 GREAT LAKES EXPO BUS, 7", 1936. This toy was also made in a larger size. D

3780 NEW YORK WORLD'S FAIR BUS, 10 1/2", 1939-1940. This toy has a nickel plated separate radiator in the rear and a nickel plated decorative piece on the roof. It was made in three sizes. This one is the largest. E

A page from a 1940 catalog showing the three sizes of New York's World Fair buses that Arcade sold in 1939/1940.

Page from a 1940 Arcade catalog showing the New York World's Fair Tractor-train toys.

727 NEW YORK WORLD'S FAIR TRACTOR-TRAIN, 7 1/4", 1939-1940. This toy was made for the 1939/40 World's Fair. The tractor has a nickel plated driver. D

729 NEW YORK WORLD'S FAIR TRACTOR-TRAIN, 16 1/2", 1939-1940. The tractor has a nickel plated driver. F

TRUCKS

202 FORD STAKE TRUCK, 9", 1926-1930. The very scarce Ford Model T Stake Truck has a cast-in bed. It came with a nickel plated driver. G

*FORD STAKE BODY TRUCK, 9", 1927-1928. This Model T Ford Truck came with a nickel plated driver. F

*CHEVROLET UTILITY EXPRESS TRUCK, 9", 1925-1928. Came with a nickeled driver. F

*FORD STAKE BODY TRUCK, 8 3/4", 1925-1927. Came equipped with a nickel plated driver. It is shown in a 1926 Arcade ad and misidentified as a Chevrolet Utility Truck. F

204 FORD ANTHONY DUMP TRUCK, 8 1/2", 1925-1927. This toy didn't come with a driver and had a spring-operated dump bed with "Anthony Company, Streator, Ill." on the tailgate. G

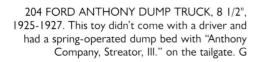

*FORD WRECKER, 11", 1926-1928. Equipped with a nickel plated driver and "Weaver" wrecker boom. This is a Model T Ford. G

*FORD ONE TON TRUCK, 8 1/2", 1923-1928. This truck has advertising for the Walsh Motor Car Company on the roof of the cab. It came with a nickel plated driver. F

203 FORD STAKE TRUCK, 6 3/4", 1926-1928. D

218 FORD WRECKER, 4 1/4", 1930-1932. C

215 FORD WRECKER, 11", 1929-1933. Equipped with a nickel plated driver and a "Weaver" wrecker boom. This is a Model A Ford. E

219 FORD DUMP TRUCK, 7 1/4", 1929-1932. This Model A Ford truck did not come with a driver. D

206 FORD STAKE TRUCK, 7 1/2", 1929-1932. This Model A Ford truck came with a nickel plated driver. D

234 FORD DUMP TRUCK
TRAILER, 13 1/2"; 280 SIDE DUMP
TRAILER, 7 1/2", 1931-1932. Came
with a nickel plated driver. G; E

217 FORD WRECKER, 7", 1929.
Came with a separate boom. D

220 FORD DUMP TRUCK,
5 3/4", 1930-1932. C

208 FORD STAKE TRUCK,
5 3/4", 1929-1934. C

213 FORD STAKE TRUCK, 4 3/4", 1929-1933. B

3050 FORD WRECKER, 4 1/2", 1933-1934. B

2010 FORD STAKE TRUCK, 6 1/2", 1933.
Came with a nickel plated grill. D

2020 FORD WRECKER, 6 3/4", 1933-1936.
Came with a nickel plated grill and winch. D

A page from an Arcade catalog.

216 RED BABY WRECKER, 12", 1926-1932. This toy came with a nickel plated driver and a "Weaver" wrecker boom. In later years it came with the 458 Two Wheel Jack. F

211 RED BABY DUMP TRUCK, 10 3/4", 1926-1928. For several years the Red Baby Dump Truck came with "International" stamped in black on each side of the dump bed. E

211 RED BABY DUMP TRUCK, 10 3/4", 1929-1935. The toy shown has black rubber tires and was probably one of the last made. E

211 YELLOW BABY DUMP TRUCK, 10 3/4".
This scarce version of the International Baby
Dump Truck was made for a brief period of time
and was not found in any Arcade catalog. It came
with a nickel plated driver, hoist, and winch. H

A 212 RED BABY STATIONARY TRUCK, 10",
1926-1931. Has International shield on each door
and came with a nickel plated driver. F

226 INTERNATIONAL DELIVERY TRUCK,
9 1/2", 1932-1935. Came with a nickel
plated driver and opening rear door. G

226 INTERNATIONAL DELIVERY TRUCK, 9 1/2",
1932-1935. Came with a nickel plated driver
attached to the door and a hinged rear door with
latch. A large private order of these trucks was
made for the Hathaway Bakery with their logo. G

237 INTERNATIONAL STAKE TRUCK, 12",
1931-1935. Came with a nickel plated driver. G

309 INTERNATIONAL STAKE TRUCK, 11 3/4",
1936-1939. Came with a nickel plated grill. G

302 INTERNATIONAL DELIVERY
TRUCK, 9 1/2", 1936-1939. Came
with a nickel plated grill. I

303 INTERNATIONAL DUMP TRUCK, 10 1/4",
1936-1939. Came with a nickel plated grill. G

260 INTERNATIONAL STAKE TRUCK, 9 1/2",
1938-1940. Came with a nickel plated grill. G

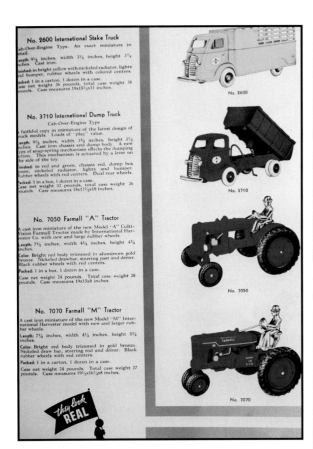

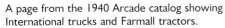

A page from the 1940 Arcade catalog showing
International trucks and Farmall tractors.

710 INTERNATIONAL DUMP TRUCK, 11". Not found in available
catalogs but believed to have been made in late 1941. E

700 INTERNATIONAL PICKUP TRUCK, 9
1/2". Not found in available catalogs but
believed to have been made in late 1941. E

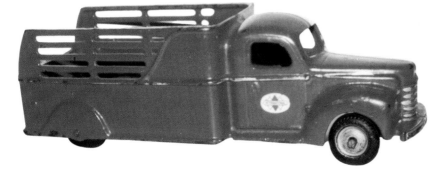

709 INTERNATIONAL STAKE TRUCK, 11 1/2".
Not found in available catalogs but believed to
have been made in late 1941. E

228 YELLOW CAB PANEL DELIVERY TRUCK, 8 1/4",
1925-1929. Has a nickel plated driver and side-
mounted spare tire. This was proclaimed in Arcade ads
as a new member of the Toy Yellow Cab family. H

66

252 WHITE AMBULANCE, 8 1/4", 1929-1930. Came with a nickel plated driver and no rear door. This is extremely scarce painted as an ambulance. J

Page from a 1929 catalog showing Arcade's great line of WHITE vehicles.

249 WHITE DUMP TRUCK, 11 1/2", 1929-1931. Came with a nickel plated driver. This is a scarce and very desirable toy. It was made in solid colors in 1930-1931. I

1933 ICE TRUCK, 6 3/4". This toy can't be found in any available Arcade catalogs but was probably made about 1937-1938. Came with imitation cakes of ice and ice tongs. We know it is Number 1933 because one was found in its original labeled box. D

280 STAKE TRUCK, 6 3/4", 1932-1935. Came with nickel plated wheels. This truck was only available in a boxed set and is unusual because it isn't marked Arcade. D

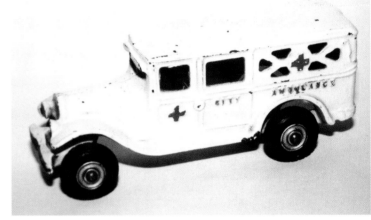

188 AMBULANCE, 6", 1932-1940. Also came painted in blue and in various boxed sets through 1940. D

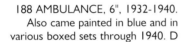

2977 TRANSPORT AND FOUR VE-HICLES, 11 1/2", 1938-1940. This toy was also made in a larger size. E

297 CARRY CAR TRAILER, 14", 1931-1934. This set actually came with a coupe, a van, and a stake truck, all Austins. F

240 CARRY CAR TRAILER, 24 1/2" 1932. To be totally correct, this car carrier should have two Sedans and two Coupes. H

223 MACK DUMP TRUCK, 12 1/4",
1926-1931. This early version of the Mack
dump truck had a decal on the hood and a
Bulldog decal on each side of the cab. F

223 MACK DUMP TRUCK, 12 1/4", 1932. This
toy came with a nickel plated driver and the
name "Mack" in raised letters on each door. E

223 MACK DUMP TRUCK, 12 1/4", 1932-
1939. This truck has the painted spoked
wheels while ones produced in later years
had rubber tires with painted centers. E

Left: Note the details, the driver and chains on the tires. (Toy never came with chains.)

A page from a 1932 Arcade catalog.

*MACK STAKE TRUCK. This toy was made from a Mack dump truck by some enterprising individual. The stake bed is made of wood and probably was in the office of the C. D. Kline Transfer Line. E

33 MACK LUBRITE GASOLINE TRUCK, 13", 1925-1929. This is a fairly scarce version of the No. 33 tank truck. It has a nickel plated driver and static arresting chain like the real ones had. H

241X MACK GASOLINE TANK TRUCK, 12 3/4", 1930-1941. The tank can be filled with water, which can then be drained from a rubber hose at the rear of the tank. G

Large Arcade cars and trucks were frequently available with either cast iron wheels or with rubber tires (at a slight additional cost). Some trucks, as the years went by, were equipped with nickel plated or painted cast iron wheels, then with cast iron wheels with white rubber tires, white rubber tires with painted centers, and, finally, by 1935, with black rubber tires and painted centers. By the late 1930s, most tires were made of black rubber; however, some toys still had white rubber tires in 1941. Also Arcade actually painted some white tires black. Many tractors made during the late 1930s and early 1940s have front tires that are painted black over white rubber.

257 MACK ICE TRUCK, 10 1/2", 1930-1935. This toy came with a nickel plated driver, ice tongs, and three pieces of imitation ice. It also came with a removable end gate, which is frequently missing. G

255 MACK WRECKER, 12 1/2", 1930-1932. This truck, with its operating "Weaver" wrecker boom, has a nickel plated driver, an opening tool box, and came with a two-wheel jack. Today the "Two-Wheel Jack 458" is a very scarce item. G

458 TWO WHEEL JACK, 5 1/2", 1931-1932. Was included with the large International and Mack Wreckers but could also be bought separately. It is quite scarce. C

246 MACK MILK TRUCK , 11 1/4", 1929-1932. This is a very scarce toy rarely found with its original four milk cans. In 1932 it was known as the Mack Milk Truck and came as shown with four milk cans. Prior to that it was called a Mack Stake Truck and didn't come with cans. H

244 MACK HIGH DUMP, 10", 1932-1940. Came with a nickeled driver, a load of imitation coal, and cast iron nickel plated shovel. It also came with a loose partition for the dump bed. Most were painted red. Green is very unusual. G

245 MACK CHEMICAL TRUCK, 15" (to the end of ladders), 1926-1930. This truck came with a nickel plated driver, a nickel plated hose reel, a hose, and two ladders. Apparently few were made as this is the most difficult of the large Arcade Mack Trucks to find. It was also made in a 9 3/4" size. I

242 MACK FIRE TRUCK, 21" (to the end of the ladders), 1926-1940. This truck was equipped with a nickel plated driver, 5 nickel plated ladder racks with a hose reel, a bell, a hose, two extension ladders, and two non-extension ladders. This toy was quite popular and many are still available. F

253 MACK STAKE TRUCK, 8 3/4", 1929-1933. Came with a nickeled driver. In 1933 it came with a Holstein Cow Bank. E

200 PONTIAC WRECKER, 4 1/4", 1936. Came with a nickel plated grill and hood trim. C

239 PONTIAC STAKE TRUCK, 6 1/4", 1936-1940. Came with a nickel plated grill and hood trim. D

2620 CHEVROLET DELIVERY TRUCK, 3 3/4", 1936-1938. This toy has a separate chassis and a nickel plated grill. C

2630 CHEVROLET WRECKER, 4", 1936-1938. This toy has a separate chassis and a nickel plated grill. C

6990 FIRE ENGINE, 13 1/4", 1941. It has a nickel plated hose reel and a hose and came with a bell. E

262 CHEVROLET AMBULANCE, 3 3/4", 1939-1941. This was only sold as part of the SOLDIER and WARFARE SET No. 688. C

1493 WRECKER TRUCK, 6", 1938-1941. Equipped with a nickel plated boom. C

1503 WRECKER TRUCK, 4 3/4", 1938-1941. Equipped with a nickel plated boom. B

1740 FIRE ENGINE, 8 3/4", 1936-1940. This has a nickel plated grill, and the catalog notes that the toy has a Pontiac grill and hood trim. D

2350 FIRE LADDER TRUCK, 4 3/4", 1936-1941. B; 2340 Fire Engine, 4 1/2", 1936-1941. B. In 1941 they came with the Fire House and had black rubber tires as shown. They both have nickeled Pontiac-like grills.

A page from an Arcade catalog.

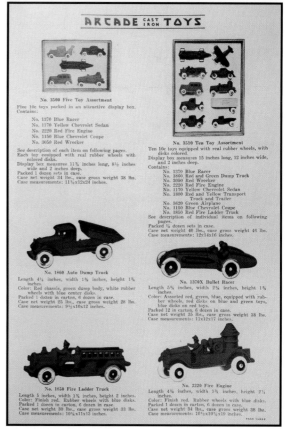

A page from an Arcade catalog.

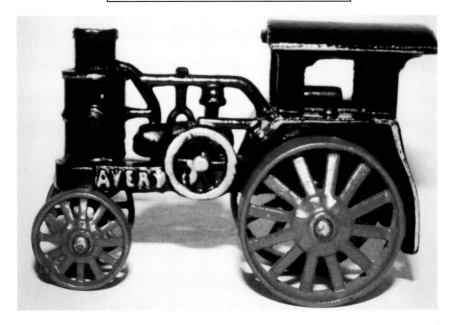

*AVERY TRACTOR,
4 1/2", 1923-1925. D

*AVERY TRACTOR, 4 1/2", 1926-
1928. Came in gray or green. D

275-3 FORDSON TRACTOR,
5 3/4", 1923-1933. Came with
a nickel plated driver and lug
rear wheels. D

275-1 FORDSON TRACTOR,
5 3/4", 1923-1929. This tractor
had no lugs on its rear
wheels—lugs make marks on
the hardwood floors. Came
with a nickel plated driver.
Arcade made far less of this
smooth wheel version than the
one with lug wheels. D

275-7 FORDSON TRACTOR, 5 3/4", 1929-1934. The early Arcade Ford tractors were painted gray. The later ones were red with green wheels or green with red wheels. They all had nickel plated drivers. D

0 W & K TRACTOR, 5 3/4", 1923-1930. This Fordson Tractor with its large rubber-tired disc wheels copied the Whitehead and Kales Industrial Tractor used in large factories. D

Detail of W & K Tractor box.

279 MCCORMICK-DEERING FARMALL, 6", 1929-1938. It has a nickel plated drawbar and steering frame. E

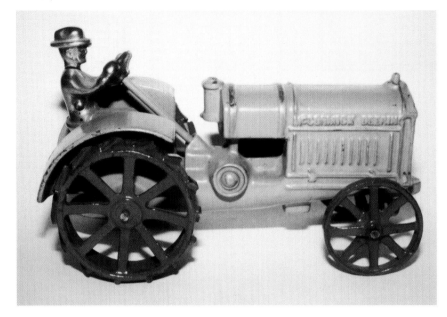

276-3 MCCORMICK-DEERING TRACTOR, 7 1/4", 1925-1939. This is a model of the McCormick-Deering 1020 tractor and it came with a nickel plated driver. D

7200 TRACTOR, 6 1/2", 1940-1941. E ; 4230 Oliver Plow, 6 1/4", 1940-1941. C. This is a model of the Ford tractor. The driver is cast-in. The plow was sold separately and is stamped "Oliver."

7300 TRACTOR WITH LOAD AND DUMP TRAILER, 15 1/4", 1941. This represents a late 1930s Ford Tractor with a trailer that has an opening bottom. E

7220 FORD TRACTOR AND PLOW, 8 1/2", 1941. The plow is attached to the rear of the tractor and can be raised and lowered by a lever. F

274 FORDSON TRACTOR, 4 1/2", 1928-1934. B

7070 FARMALL "M" TRACTOR, 7 1/4", 1940-1941.
Came with a nickel plated driver and drawbar. D

284 TRACTOR, 5 1/2", 1936-1939.
Came in assorted colors. C

A page from the 1940 Arcade
catalog showing farm toys.

7050 FARMALL "A" "CULTI-VISION" TRAC-
TOR, 7 1/4", 1940-1941. Came with a nickel
plated driver and drawbar. E

3740 ALLIS-CHALMERS "WC" TRAC-
TOR, 7 1/4", 1940-1941. Came with a
nickel plated driver. D

*JOHN DEERE TRACTOR, 7 1/2", production
dates unknown. Came with a nickel plated
driver. Many copies of this toy have been made
in aluminum. It is interesting that this toy
doesn't appear in Arcade catalogs. D

356 OLIVER 70 ROW-CROP TRACTOR, 7 1/4",
1937-1941. Came with a nickel plated driver.
Most of these are found painted red. D

240 TRACTOR, 3", 1940-1941. B

269 CATERPILLAR TRACTOR, 6 3/4", 1931.
This toy was made in 6 sizes in 1932. It has a
nickel plated driver and chain treads. F

268 CATERPILLAR TRACTOR, 5 1/2",
1931-1934. Came with chain link track
and a nickel plated driver. E

7120 TRAC-TRACTOR-T.D. MODEL, 7 1/2", 1940-
1941. Came with a nickel plated driver. G

270 CATERPILLAR DIESEL TRACTOR, 7 3/4", 1936-1941. This
toy has an exposed engine, a nickel plated driver, and nickel
plated radiator guard. The toy pictured was a special order and
has a painted driver and seat. G

272 CATERPILLAR TRACTOR-DIESEL TYPE,
7 3/4", 1930-1934. The toy pictured was one
of Arcade's special order items. It was
stamped "Caterpillar" with "Diesel" stamped
on the radiator guard. "Ten" in raised letters
had been removed from the radiator sides. H

277 INTERNATIONAL TRAC-TRACTOR, 8", 1937-1939. Came with nickel plated steel tracks and a nickel plated driver. It was also available with rubber tracks. G

451 MCCORMICK-DEERING THRESHER, 12", 1927-1941. Has a nickel plated feeder, stack, and pulleys that revolve. Came only in gray with red pulleys and later with nickel plated pulleys. D

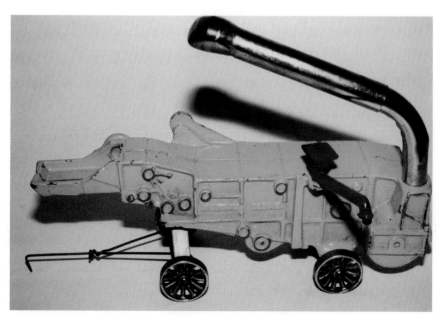

450 MCCORMICK-DEERING THRESHER, 9", 1929-1941. Came in red, green, and blue with nickel plated parts. In 1940 it was only available in yellow. D

4210 HAY MOWER, 4", 1939-1941. Generally came with black rubber tires. B

283 MCCORMICK-DEERING PLOW, 7 3/4", 1926-1941. This plow is the nicest of the Arcade plows but is usually found with levers broken off. D

282 OLIVER PLOW, 6 1/2", 1926-1939. This plow came with nickel plated wheels. The catalogs don't mention that it came in green as well as red. C

4230 OLIVER PLOW, 6 1/4",
1940-1941. B

282 OLIVER PLOW, 6 1/2", 1926-1939. "Oliver" is
stamped on the moldboard. This one is completely
painted red while most have nickel plated wheels. C

402-2 MCCORMICK-DEERING SPREADER, 15", 1932-
1941. This toy works like the real one. It was made in the
late 1920s and marketed with the horses attached. In 1932-
1941 it was sold without the horses but they could be
bought separately. D

7140 OLIVER SUPERIOR SPREADER, 10",
1940-1941. This toy has three rotating shafts
to work like the real machine. E

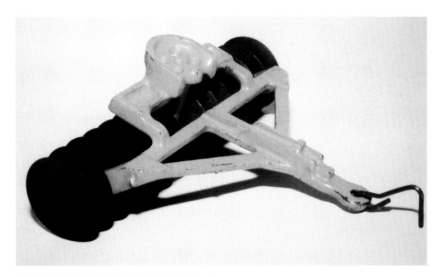

409 DISC HARROW, 3 1/2", 1938-1941. A

704 TANDEM DISC HARROW, 6 3/4", 1939-1941.
This is a hard piece of Arcade farm equipment to
find especially with all its discs. C

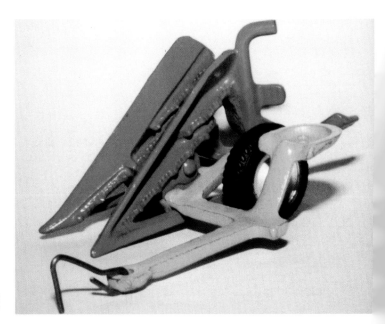

4180 CORN HARVESTER,
5", 1939-1941. C

702 CORN HARVESTER, 6 1/2", 1939-1941. C

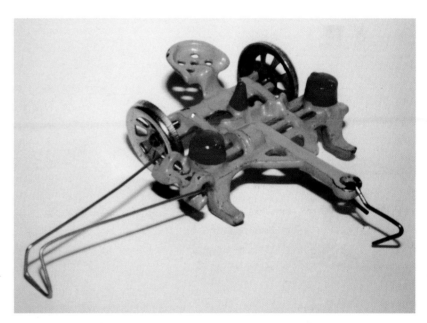

4220 CORN PLANTER,
4 1/2", 1939-1941. A

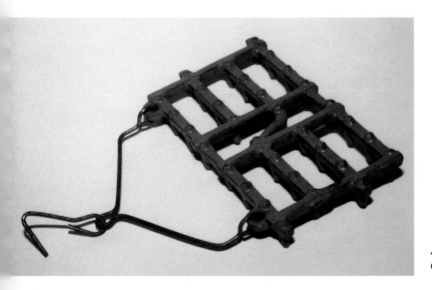

419 DRAG HARROW, 3 3/4", 1939-1941.
Only sold in the 686 FARM SET. A

417 HAY RAKE, 3 1/2", 1939-1941. Came with steel rakes and nickel plated wheels. B

*W&K TRUCK TRAILER, 8 1/2", 1923-1928. This toy trailer with Whitehead and Kales in raised letters has a pivoting front axle and 8 removable side stake racks. D

585 PUMP, 4", 1902-1932. A

289 TRAILER, 3 3/4", 1929-1932. Came with nickel plated stamped steel wheels. A

*FAIRBANKS-MORSE GAS ENGINE, 4", 1926. C

288 TRAILER, 4 1/2", 1929-1933. B

286 TRAILER, 6 1/4", 1929-1932. This trailer has a pivoting front axle but doesn' t have removable stake racks. C

408 FARM WAGON AND TEAM, 11 1/4", 1933-1937. Like 404 but the box is not removable from the gear and the seat is cast on the box. D

404-1 MCCORMICK-DEERING WEBER WAGON WITH HORSES, 11", 1927-1941. This wagon, which has a removable seat and horses that can be unbolted, was sold with or without horses. The box is removable from the gear. E

4080 FARM WAGON AND TEAM OF HORSES, 11", 1940-1941. This wagon came with a painted figure bolted-on and nickel plated chains from the horses to the double tree. D

404-5 HORSES FOR WEBER WAGON, 4 3/4", 1927-1941. Arcade sold the team of horses separately to be used with farm equipment. C

4121 DUMP WAGON AND TEAM, 13", 1941. This wagon came with a painted driver and two nickel plated tools. A lever could be moved causing the wagon bottom to open. D

290 AUSTIN ROLL-A-PLANE, 7 1/2", 1928. This scarce toy was equipped with an 8 piece nickel plated roller mechanism, probably too costly to economically produce. It was replaced by the less complicated Austin Autocrat (291). F

287 WHEEL SCRAPER, 8 1/4", 1929-1932. C

AIRPLANES

357 MONOCOUPE AIRPLANE, 9 1/2", 1929-1932. Has a nickel plated engine and propeller. The wing is made of steel. F

354 MONOCOUPE AIRPLANE, 5 3/4", 1929-1932. Came with nickel plated wheels, engine, and propeller. D

3640 AIRPLANE, 7 1/2", 1941. This toy has steel
wings and propeller with a cast iron fuselage. C

361 BOEING UNITED AIRPLANE, 3 1/2", 1936-
1941. This little airplane has a nickel plated lower
fuselage, and nickel plated steel propellers. B

BOXED SETS AND MISCELLANEOUS TOYS

772 MIDGET MODERN MA-
RINES, 1940-1941. A

400 ARMY TANK WITH GUN, 8", 1937-
1941. Came with a rubber track and a
cannon that would shoot steel balls. D

477 HAND TRUCK, 5", 1902-1930. A

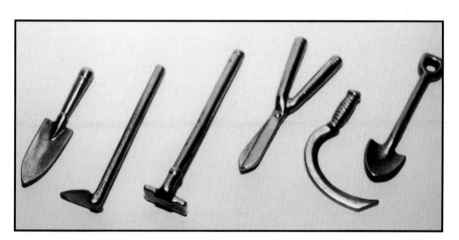

599 MIDGET GARDEN TOOLS, 1940-1941. A

787 CARDED TOY GARAGE SET, 1940-1941. B

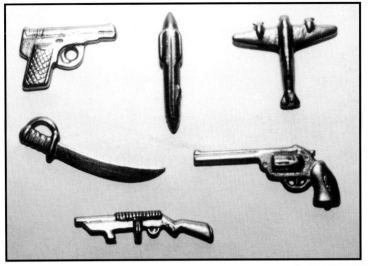

778 MIDGET ARMY TOOLS, 1940-1941. A

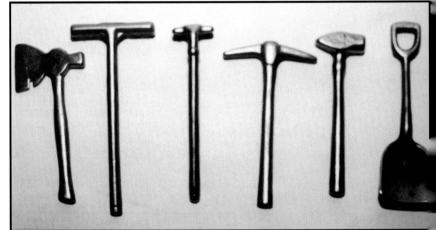

600 MIDGET TOOLS, 1902-1941. A

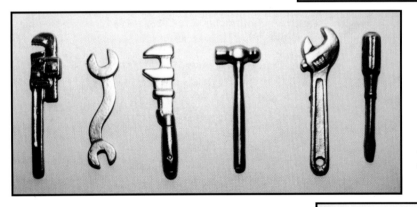

779 MIDGET MECHANICS
TOOLS, 1940-1941. B

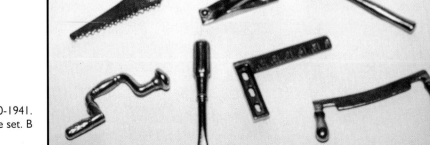

782 MIDGET CARPENTERS TOOLS, 1940-1941.
The screw driver was not part of the set. B

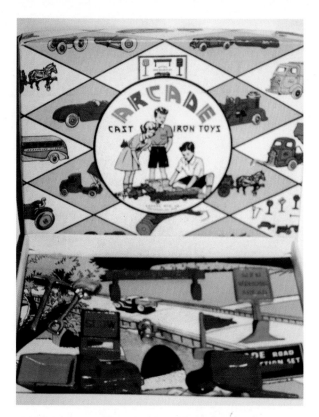

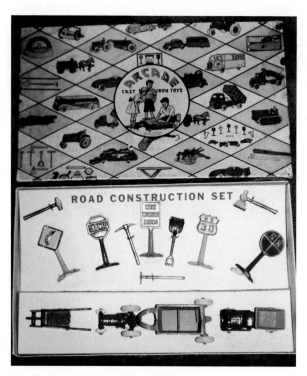

4329 ROAD CONSTRUCTION SET, 1940-1941. D

431 ROAD CONSTRUCTION SET, 1937. F

The Arcade Company had one of the most successful advertising campaigns to initiate children into the Arcade fan club. Their motto was "They Look Real." One of their most popular promotions was the booklet with a story about "Fred and Jane with the Tiny Arcadians." The 1933 Arcade catalog promoted the 16 page booklet containing "a beautiful fairy tale story about Fred and Jane and their pleasant experiences with the 'Tiny Arcadians,' a fairy folk who are the makers of Arcade Cast Iron Toys." (The name Arcadia, the name for a mythological paradise, was a popular concept in Victorian times.)

2. DENT

The Dent Hardware company was founded in Fullerton, a small town outside of Allentown, Pennsylvania, by Henry H. Dent, an English immigrant who came to this country in 1866. Dent had spent his childhood in Newark, New Jersey, before moving to Allentown, in 1889, where he worked as a bookkeeper for the Allentown Hardware Company.

In 1895, he and four partners—Henry Newhard, Charles Kaiser, C.W. Wackernagel, and George H. Brightbill—formed their own company, the Dent Hardware Company and began to manufacture refrigeration hardware and devices. In 1898 the company decided to diversify and make cast iron toys. By 1901 the company's horse-drawn vehicles were becoming a popular seller and their toys were known for their high quality and detail. The company was also the first to make

aluminum toys. At the height of its productivity the compan had more than 400 workers. However, by 1937, the com pany stopped making cast iron and aluminum toys. Due to th high cost of tooling these toys, the company was unable t remain competitive with the cheaper die cast and stampe steel toys.

In 1956 the partnership dissolved, and the Dent fami sold their interest to the Newhard family who continued t make refrigerator and cold storage hardware. The Dent fami organized a new company, Dent Manufacturing Incorporate On November 23, 1973, the Dent Hardware Company wa finally dissolved, and on January 20, 1974, all the conten and equipment of the company were sold at auction.

There is an interesting postscript to the story. In 194

Richard Dent, the grandson of Henry H., discovered a hidden cache of toys wrapped in newspapers from 1903 in a large closet on the third floor of the factory. Apparently they had been put away years ago and forgotten. Richard Dent unwrapped the toys—there were hundreds of them—and lined them up on benches. Overjoyed he told his father about his discovery. His father believed these toys were destroyed and the materials used for the war effort. Upon seeing the toys, his eyes filled with tears.

Dent took home a few toys, leaving the others wrapped and packed away in a large paint oven, which he padlocked. Years later when he returned to claim them, they were gone. By the time he returned more than thirty years had passed, and the Newhards had sold the toys to several individuals.

The Dent Hardware factory still stands in the small neighborhood of Fullerton, a few miles outside of Allentown. It is now rented by a group of small businesses. But even in the 1970s and 1980s curious treasure seeking toy collectors were still able to find old boxes, labels, and bits and pieces of old toys around the factory.

We have not been able to date Dent toys precisely because there are only two catalogs and neither were dated.

MAIN OFFICE AND FACTORIES
THE DENT HARDWARE COMPANY
FULLERTON, PENNA.

AUTOMOBILES

*EARLY TOURING CAR, 8 1/2", probably made prior to World War I but not found in the catalogs. F

*TOURING CAR, 9 1/4", probably made during the 1920s. This car has a unique feature, a man and woman in the rear seat. D

1920s TOURING CAR, 12", similar to the smaller 1920s touring car. F

AMOS and ANDY FRESH AIR TAXI, 6". This and the Toonerville Trolley are the only two toys that Dent made based on popular comic strips. E

618 COUPE, 6 1/4". This toy was based on a Model T Ford. E

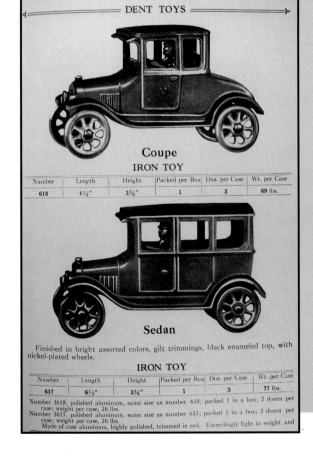

=== DENT TOYS ===

Coupe
IRON TOY

Number	Length	Height	Packed per Box	Doz. per Case	Wt. per Case
618	6¼"	3¾"	1	3	69 lbs.

Sedan

Finished in bright assorted colors, gilt trimmings, black enameled top, with nickel-plated wheels.

IRON TOY

Number	Length	Height	Packed per Box	Doz. per Case	Wt. per Case
617	6½"	3¾"	1	3	77 lbs.

Number 3618, polished aluminum, same size as number 618; packed 1 in a box; 2 dozen per case; weight per case, 26 lbs.
Number 3617, polished aluminum, same size as number 617; packed 1 in a box; 2 dozen per case; weight per case, 26 lbs.
Made of cast aluminum, highly polished, trimmed in red. Exceedingly light in weight and

A page from a Dent catalog.

632 SEDAN, 5 1/2" B

706 SPORT ROADSTER, 5 3/4". Came with two passengers in the rumble seat. This was a unique feature. D

The letter R, following the toy's model number, is used in this chapter to mean equipped with rubber tires. The catalog number of each toy is included whenever possible. Where there is an *, it means that there is no catalog number available. Since Dent did not date its catalogs nor its supplements, it is difficult to date Dent toys.

641R ROADSTER, 4 3/4". B

*ROADSTER, 4 3/4". B

*SEDAN, 4 3/4". B

*SEDAN, 4 3/4". Made of aluminum. B

This 8" sedan came out of the Dent sample room. It was made by Kenton and apparently was purchased by Dent for comparison to their no. 669, 8" Sedan. Dent painted it red with a black roof probably to better judge it against a similarly painted Dent.

669 SEDAN, 7 3/4". D

731 CHRYSLER AIRFLOW FASTBACK COUPES, 5 3/4" with the box. The original box contained a half dozen. The cars were made just prior to Dent ceasing toy production in 1937. They have a nickeled grill. D

271 TAXICAB, 8". Has a license plate with the number 543. D

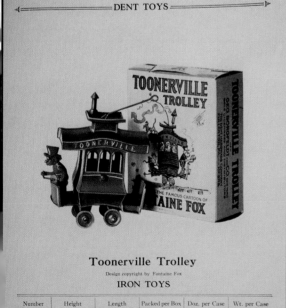

Left:
The TOONERVILLE TROLLEY shown in No. 10 Dent catalog.

Right:
50 TOONERVILLE TROLLEY, 5 3/4". This is a model of the celebrated Toonerville Trolley originated by Fontaine Fox. It is furnished with the Skipper and runs on eccentric wheels which gives it an erratic rocking motion when rolled along. D

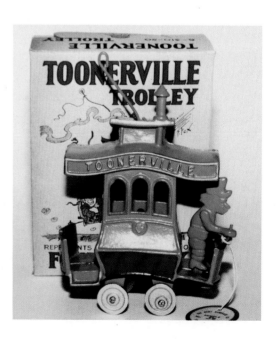

671 PUBLIC SERVICE BUS, 14 1/4". Has a separate rear mounted spare. This toy is probably an updated version of the PUBLIC SERVICE BUS, which is slightly shorter, but has a considerably higher roof. F

PUBLIC SERVICE BUS, 13 3/4". Has a separate driver and a rear mounted spare. H

COAST TO COAST BUS, 15 1/4". Has a separate driver. H

1670 INTERURBAN BUS, 9". Made of aluminum. D

648 TWIN MOTOR
COACH, 10 1/4". E

670R INTERURBAN BUS, 9" E

619 INTERURBAN BUS, 5" B

BUS, 8". Looks like an
early school bus. D

683 INTERURBAN BUS, 6", 1920s. C

TRUCKS

688 MACK CONTRACTOR'S TRUCK, 10 3/4". This toy has a riveted-in driver and is equipped with three mechanically operated buckets. F

277 MACK JUNIOR SUPPLY COMPANY VAN, 15 3/4". The back doors open and the truck has a separate driver and steering wheel. H

278 MACK TANK TRUCK,
15 1/2". Has separate driver
and steering wheel. H

276 MACK DUMP TRUCK, 15 1/2". Has a separate
driver, steering wheel, and pull cord with cast ring. H

279 MACK FLAT BED TRUCK, 15 3/4". Has a separate driver, steering
wheel and removable stakes, and chain and pull cord with cast ring. H

A page from the Dent catalog.

DENT TOYS

Air Express—Tri-Motor Aeroplane

A new cabin design with triple motor, burnished nickel-plated finish. Propellers highly polished nickel. Finished in bright colors with red and gilt trimmings. Nickel-plated disc wheels with red centers. An exact reproduction of the latest model aeroplanes.

IRON TOY

Number	Length	Wing Spread	Packed per Box	Doz. per Case	Wt. per Case
652	11"	11½"	1	1	50 lbs.

Number 2652, polished aluminum, same size as number 652; made of cast aluminum, highly polished with polished propellers; trimmed in red, with disc wheels. Very light in weight, attractive in appearance; packed 1 in a box; 1 dozen per case; weight per case, 30 lbs.

Mack Motor Fire Truck

A very accurate reproduction of the Mack Fire Trucks, made up in bright red with gilt trimmings, highly polished nickel-plated wheels with red centers, dual wheels in rear. Equipped with two 10" wood ladders, hose reel, nozzle and two suction rubber pipes.

IRON TOY

Number	Length	Height	Packed per Box	Doz. per Case	Wt. per Case
600	15"	6"	1	1	86 lbs.

600 MACK PIONEER FIRE TRUCK, 15". This toy has a separate driver with separate steering wheel, two wood ladders, hose reel, and two suction hoses. It also has its pull cord with cast iron ring. G

665 DUMP TRUCK, 5" C.

Right:
695R MACK DUMP TRUCK, 4 1/4". C

Dent made an absolutely wonderful series of five large Mack trucks consisting of a Dump truck, Tank truck, Flat Bed truck, Junior Supply Company van, and a Pioneer Fire truck. They are all 15 inches long. The castings are very fine and the detail is great.

1295 MACK DUMP TRUCK, 5 1/4". Made of aluminum with cast-in driver and nickel plated disc wheels. Although it was called a dump truck in the catalog, it has a fixed bed and can't dump. C

697R AUTO WRECKING CAR, 5". C

1697 AUTO WRECKING CAR, 5". Made of aluminum with nickel plated stamped wheels. B

684 TANK TRUCK, 5 3/4" C

1684 TANK TRUCK, 5 3/4". Made of aluminum
with stamped and nickel plated disc wheels. B

720 AUTO EXPRESS TRUCK, 4 1/2". Has stamped steel nickel plated wheels. B

*AUTO EXPRESS TRUCK, 5". This long bed
version of 720 is not found in the catalogs. C

*CONTRACTOR'S TRUCK, 8 3/4". Has a
riveted-in driver and three dumping bins. F

Dent packing labels.

Auto Bus
1-12 Doz.   No. 620
Manufactured by
THE DENT HARDWARE CO.
FULLERTON, PA., U. S. A.

Motor Coach
PAINTED
1-12 DOZ.   No. 648
Manuf. by The Dent Hardware Co.
Fullerton, Pa., U. S. A.

COMBINATION
Fire Truck
1-12 DOZ.   No. 299
Manuf. by The Dent Hardware Co.
Fullerton, Pa., U. S. A.

Hook & Ladder
1-12 Doz.   No. 606
MADE IN U. S. A.

" LUCKY BOY "
AEROPLANE
PAINTED
½ DOZ.   No. 65o
Manufactured by The Dent Hardware Co.
Fullerton, Pa., U. S. A., Reg. U. S. pat. Office

Large Airplane
½ Doz.   No. 643
Manufactured by
THE DENT HARDWARE CO.
FULLERTON, PA., U. S. A.

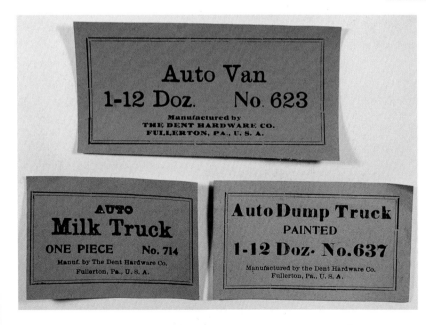

Auto Van
1-12 Doz.   No. 623
Manufactured by
THE DENT HARDWARE CO.
FULLERTON, PA., U. S. A.

AUTO
Milk Truck
ONE PIECE   No. 714
Manuf. by The Dent Hardware Co.
Fullerton, Pa., U. S. A.

Auto Dump Truck
PAINTED
1-12 Doz. No. 637
Manufactured by the Dent Hardware Co.
Fullerton, Pa., U. S. A.

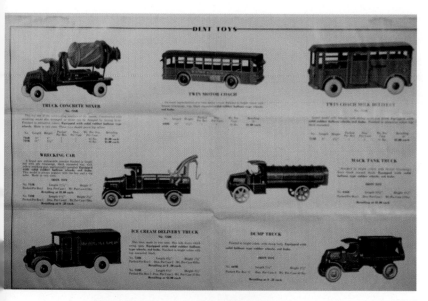

From the Dent fold-out which includes the now very scarce Concrete Mixer Truck.

687 WRECKING CAR, 10 1/4". Driver is riveted to the door. F

713R TWIN COACH MILK DELIV-ERY VAN, 8". This toy has a standing driver and two sliding doors. E

723R BREYERS ICE CREAM DELIVERY TRUCK, 8 1/2". This toy has three opening doors on the right side and the name "Breyers Ice Cream" on the left. G

686 POLICE PATROL VAN, 8 1/4". Has a driver riveted to door and a side mounted spare tire. H

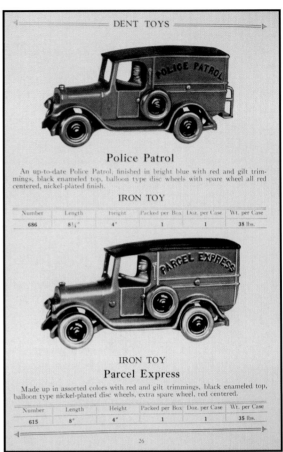

A page from a Dent catalog showing two very desirable vans from the No. 10 Dent catalog.

615 PARCEL EXPRESS VAN, 8". Has a driver riveted to door and side mounted spare tire. H

268 HOOK and LADDER, 14 3/4". E

208 FIRE ENGINE, 10 1/2". E

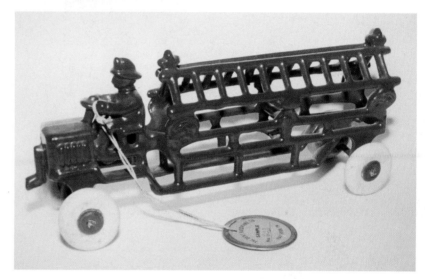

602 HOOK and LADDER, 6 3/4".
Has a Dent sample room tag on it. C

FARM EQUIPMENT

646 TRACTOR, 5". C

638 TRACTOR, 3 3/4". B

638R TRACTOR, 3 3/4". B

ROAD CONSTRUCTION EQUIPMENT

701 STREET SWEEPER, 6". The revolving brush operates by means of a sprocket and wheel. It was made in a larger size. Both are difficult to find. F

664 STEAM SHOVEL, 4 3/4". C

705 STEAM SHOVEL, 5 1/2". Revolves on its base. C

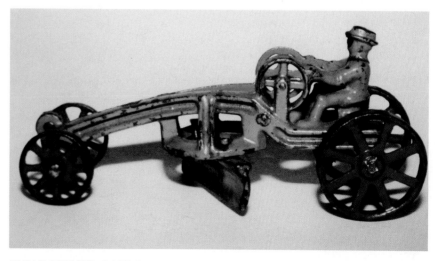

*ROAD SCRAPER, 5 1/2". B

645R ROAD ROLLER, 4 1/2". B

647 ROAD ROLLER, 6". C

718 STEAM ROLLER, 4 3/4". C

116

640R SIDE DUMP TRAILER, 4 1/2".
Has a steel dump body. A

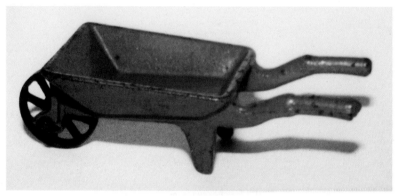

682 WHEEL BARROW, 4". A

696 HAND FREIGHT TRUCK, 4 1/4". A

*HAND TRUCK, 4 3/4"
(including wire handle). B

Box of one dozen Lucky Boy airplanes. These toys came out of the factory, where they had been stored, long after toy production had ceased in 1937. B

LUCKY BOY AIRPLANE, 4 1/2". B

LUCKY BOY AIRPLANE, 4 1/2". This is a brass pattern that was assembled into a toy possibly by a Dent factory worker. B

675 FORD TRIMOTOR AIRPLANE, 12". This toy is a faithful copy of the real Ford Trimotor that was used for years for passenger travel. Today there are still several in daily use. H

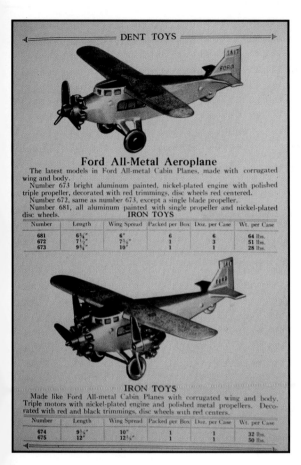

Dent's Ford all-metal cabin planes shown in the No. 10 catalog.

681R FORD ALL-METAL AIRPLANE, 6 3/4". E

659 LUCKY BOY AIRPLANE, 9 1/2". F

*LUCKY BOY TRIMOTOR AIRPLANE, 6 3/4". E

*LINDY AIRPLANE, 6 3/4". D

660R LUCKY BOY AIRPLANE, 10 3/4". G

652 AIR EXPRESS AIRPLANE, 10 3/4", equipped with three nickel plated propellers and rubber tires. H

*QUESTION MARK AIRPLANE, 10 3/4",
equipped with nickel plated engines and
three bladed propellers. H

644 ZEP DIRIGIBLE, 5". B

Also pictured is a brass
pattern of the same toy.

1644 ZEP DIRIGIBLE, 5". Made of polished
aluminum. A print block with the catalog cut
for this toy is in the background. B

654 ZEP DIRIGIBLE, 6 1/2". D

2654 ZEP DIRIGIBLE, 6 3/4".
Made of polished aluminum. C

3655 LOS ANGELES DIRIGIBLE, 8 1/2".
Made of polished aluminum. D

656 LOS ANGELES DIRIGIBLE, 12 1/2". F

BOATS

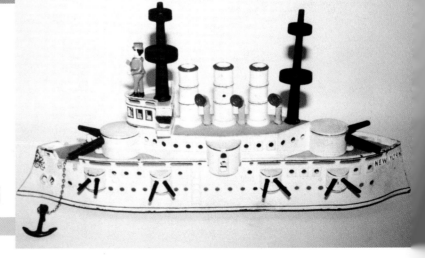

8 CRUISER NEW YORK,
20". Painted version. I

8 CRUISER NEW YORK, 20". This toy was copper flashed by the factory, a technique that was used to give the toy a unique look with patches of shiny copper on a field of a dull brownish hue. Several toy companies copper flashed some of their products and in some cases offered certain models painted, nickeled, or copper flashed. This toy was owned by Henry Newhard, one of the Dent co-founding partners, and was reported to be in his office for years. It was purchased in 1992 at an auction of his family's possessions that included many Dent toys. I

BOXED SETS

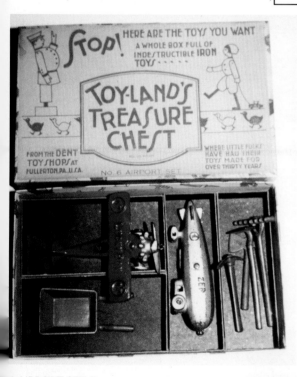

6 AIRPORT SET. F

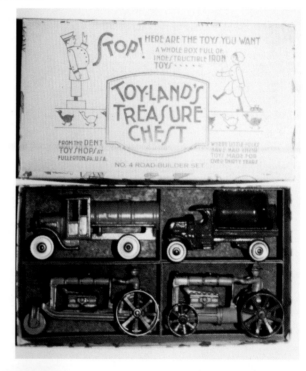

4 ROADBUILDER SET. F

TOYLAND'S TREASURE CHEST SET. F

TOYLAND'S TREASURE CHEST of
eight vehicles, one escaped. F

TOYLAND'S TREASURE CHEST of four aluminum vehicles. D

3. HUBLEY
"It's a Hubley Toy"

The Hubley company was founded in 1898 in Lancaster, Pennsylvania, by John E. Hubley. Originally the company specialized in the manufacture of toy trains. In 1909 the company was reorganized under new management, and under the leadership of John H. Hartman and Joseph T. Breneman, the company started to manufacture cast iron toys and novelties. Their first toys were horse-drawn wagons and fire engines, miniature coal stoves, horse-drawn circus wagons, and toy guns. Eventually automotive toys were added to the line. As the real automotive industry grew, Hubley tried to keep up by adding more and more models to the line. By the 1930s automotive toys dominated the company's production.

Hubley's prosperity was due to the fact that the company supplied the growing number of dime store chains with inexpensive miniature models of cars, trucks, motorcycles, and buses.

Hubley also got the exclusive rights to use such well-known brand names as Borden's®, Indian®, Harley Davidson®, Old Dutch®, Huber®, Packard®, Bell Telephone®, General Electric®, and Maytag®.

Hubley ceased its cast iron toy production in 1942 due to the growing demands of its war contracts and the need for materials to be devoted to the war effort. After the war the

company made some cast iron telephone trucks, but mostly made die cast metal and plastic toys. In 1955 the name was changed to Gabriel Industries, and in 1978 the entire operation was bought by CBS.

(Note: The Hubley catalogs sometimes use an E after the toy's number to indicate electric (battery operated) headlights.

684 AUTOMOBILE, 8 1/2", made from the teens into the mid 1920s. D

314 TAXI, 4", B ; 300 COUPE, 4", B. These were made from the mid 1920s until 1929.

309 AUTO GROCERY VAN, 3 3/4", B; LIMOUSINE 4", B—made from the teens into the mid 1920s.

664 ROADSTER, 7 1/4", produced in the early 1920s. This attractive toy is referred to as the Port-hole Coupe and was only made in one size. E

707 LINCOLN TOURING CAR, 11 3/4", made for a few years in the 1920s. This copy of a 1920 Lincoln is one of only two known to exist. J

711 LINCOLN SEDAN, 11 3/4", early 1920s. Like the touring car, this toy is extremely scarce and was made for just a few years in the early 1920s. J

665 COUPE, 6 3/4". This toy, which resembles a Dodge, was made in five sizes ranging from 4 1/4" to 9 1/2" from the mid 1920s until 1930. D

721 COUPE, 8 1/2", mid 1920s until 1930. E

710 PACKARD STRAIGHT 8 SEDAN, 11 1/2", late 1920s. Considered the best cast iron automobile made. It has opening hoods that expose the straight 8 motor, a lovely nickel plated grill, two opening doors, front and rear seats, a nickel plated driver, separate chassis, a large bumper, and twin shock absorber towers. These are very fragile toys and when found almost always are broken and have missing or replaced parts. K

Detail.

710 PACKARD STRAIGHT 8 SEDAN, 11 1/2". This toy was only made for a few years in the late 1920s. The toys were either blue, green, or red with black chassis and roofs. K

378 DELUXE STATION WAGON, 5", introduced in 1933 and offered in two series—Standard and Deluxe. The Deluxe came with dual side-mounts. These toys, which came with detachable bodies, were made with car and truck bodies. By 1934, only the Deluxe versions were still available. By 1936, they had disappeared from the Hubley catalog. C

644 STATION WAGON, 6", detachable body, circa 1933. D

643 SEDAN, 6", 1933. This standard version of the detachable body was made only in 1933. It came in 6" and 5" sizes. D

642 COUPE, 6", 1933. Like the Sedan and Roadster, this standard detachable body Coupe was made only in 1933 and came in two sizes. D

641 ROADSTER, 6", circa 1933, available in two sizes. D

*ROADSTER, 4 1/2". This series also has a Coupe, a Sedan, and a Touring Car and was probably made in 1934/1935. C

*SEDAN, 4 1/2", nickel plated grill and a separate chassis and was probably made in 1934/1935 but the 1934 catalog only shows the autos in this series to be 3 3/4". C

As car sales grew, toy makers immediately realized that a new generation of young boys wanted to "drive" too. Seeing booming sales opportunities, they began to manufacture toy versions of the most popular cars of the day. Hubley manufactured toy cars such as the Chrysler Airflow Coupe and Sedan.

701E CHRYSLER AIRFLOW, 8". Introduced in 1934, this is on of Hubley's electrical toys with battery operated headlights. features nickeled trim around the windshield and is a very nic model of the 1934 Chrysler Airflow. Like the real Chrysl Airflow, it was discontinued a few years later.

Detail of CHRYSLER headlights.

*CHRYSLER AIRFLOW SEDAN, 6 1/4", probably made in 1935. Came with nickel plated separate chassis. D

390 CHRYSLER AIRFLOW COUPE, 4 1/2", 1934 until about 1936. Came with a nickel plated separate chassis. B

625E CHRYSLER AIRFLOW TWO DOOR SEDAN, 6 1/4", with separate chassis and working headlights, probably just made during 1936. F

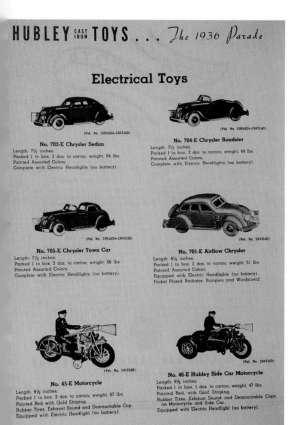

705E CHRYSLER TOWN CAR, 7 1/4", made from 1934 to about 1936. It has a separate chassis, an aluminum windshield, and working headlights. It was also made as a Sedan and as a Roadster. G

Some of Hubley's 1936 Electrical Toy offerings.

610 STUDEBAKER TOWN CAR, 6 3/4", circa 1934-1938. D

608 STUDEBAKER SEDAN, 6 3/4". The Studebaker series was made in two sizes (6 3/4" and 5") from 1934 through 1938. The cars have a nickel plated chassis with separate nickeled head lamps. D

609 STUDEBAKER ROADSTER, 6 3/4", circa 1934-1938. D

394 STUDEBAKER TOWN CAR, 5", 1934-1936, part of Hubley's Midget Line, also made 6 3/4". It has a separate chassis and a nickeled grill. C

393 STUDEBAKER SEDAN, 5", 1934-1936. It was also made 6 3/4". C

392 STUDEBAKER COUPE, 5", 1934-1936. C

391 STUDEBAKER ROADSTER, 5", 1934-1936. Also made 6 3/4". C

317 ROADSTER, 4 1/2", circa 1938. B

The "Yellow Cab Company" Taxicab, 8 1/4 inches, made during the 1920s. This is unusual as Hubley is not known for placing any names, phone numbers, or other data on their taxis as Arcade generally did.

678 TAXICAB, 6 1/4", 1920s. Cast-in driver and separate spare tire. D

754 (special order) "YELLOW CAB COMPANY" TAXICAB, 8 1/4", 1920s. This is unusual as Hubley is not known for placing any names, phone numbers, or other data on their taxis like other manufacturers such as Arcade consistently did. G

752 BROWN and WHITE TAXICAB, 8 1/4", 1920s. With separate driver. F

754 YELLOW TAXICAB, 8 1/4", 1920s. This taxi is actually painted yellow and not the color orange usually known as the Yellow Cab yellow. F

751 BLACK AND WHITE TAXICAB, 8 1/4", 1920s. F

750 RED AND BLACK TAXICAB, 8 1/4", 1920s. F

> Boxes for cast iron toys are generally plain brown with a label on one end and are very scarce. They bring a stiff price because of their rarity.

753 BLUE TAXICAB, 8 1/4", 1920s. Shown with its original box. G

Hubley made over a dozen toys with electric lights. These toys appear in the 1934 through 1936 catalogs as electrical toys and can not be found in any other Hubley catalog. (Note however that catalogs have not been found for all the years of Hubley toy production.)

Toys were manufactured in many sizes. Miniature toys, three to five inches, were usually sold in dime stores, while the larger sizes, six inches or more, were usually sold in toy stores, general stores, and department stores. Usually families, especially in smaller towns, shopped in the general store. Moms bought sewing and household goods. Dads bought tools, and children picked out a small toy. Cast iron toys became very popular because they were so sturdy and durable.

Note that most cast iron Hubley toys, like many made by other manufacturers, did not bear the maker's name.

685 YELLOW CAB, 7 3/4", 1939 to 1941. It has a separate chassis, separate driver, and a fold-down luggage rack. E

754 YELLOW TAXICAB, 8 1/4", 1920s. E

BUSES

755 COAST TO COAST BUS, 13", late 1920s.
Also made in 8 1/4" and 10" lengths. G

327 BUS, 4 3/4", 1939-1941. B

A page from the Hubley catalog.

RACERS

*RACER, 5 1/2", mid 1920s. C

137

672 GOLDEN ARROW RACER, 10 3/4". This toy, which was produced from 1931 to 1941, has Hubley's patented exhaust flame feature and exhaust clicker. The name "Hubley" is in raised letters underneath. It was also made as an 8 cylinder, 8 3/4" version. G

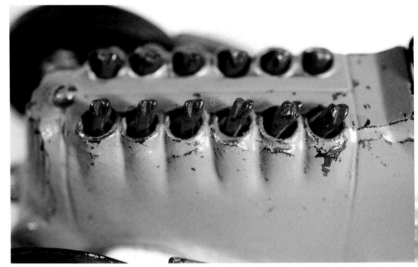

Detail of the flame exhaust feature.

677 GOLDEN ARROW RACER, 8 1/2", circa 1931-1941. This toy has the exhaust flame feature but has 8 cylinders instead of the 12 cylinders of its larger, 10 3/4" brother. E

No. 5 RED DEVIL RACER, 9 1/2". This snappy toy, as Hubley described it in the 1929 catalog, has opening hoods to expose the straight 8 cylinder engine. It was produced from 1928 until 1933 and had a polished aluminum body, nickeled chassis, and exhaust clicker. It was made in 1934 with electric lights. G

709 No. 5 AUTO RACER, 9 1/2", 1928-1936. This car has opening hoods and a straight 8 engine. It is similar to the Red Devil, but in 1929 it wholesaled for $13.50 a dozen, while the Red Devil wholesaled for $24 a dozen. F

MOTORCYCLES

399 SOLO MOTORCYCLE, 4 1/4", 1938-1941. Came with a separate cop. B

397 MOTORCYCLE, 4 1/4". 1938-1941. The rider is cast as a part of the cycle. The toy was produced in assorted colors. B

315 MOTORCYCLE, 3", part of Hubley's midget line produced in the late 1930s. A

650 2 CYLINDER HARLEY-DAVIDSON SIDECAR CYCLE, 6 1/4", from 1931 to about 1933. Wit' cast-in driver, nickel plated cast iron wheels. [

621 HARLEY-DAVIDSON MOTORCYCLE, 5 1/2", 1930 to about 1935, shown in early catalogs with Harley on the tank, but by 1934 it was shown with Harley-Davidson. The toy has nice stamped spoked wheels with white rubber tires. D

622 HARLEY-DAVIDSON HILL CLIMBER CYCLE,
5 3/4", early 1930s. It was made in two sizes. E

341 SPEED RACING CYCLE,
4 1/4". Made in the early
1930s and also made as #312
(3 1/4"). C

624E MOTORCYCLE, 6 1/4". This is a
Hubley electrical toy and may have been
made just in 1934 or possibly into 1935. D

45-E MOTORCYCLE, 8 1/2", 1934-1936. Came with a removable cop. This very scarce motorcycle was part of Hubley's series of toys with electric lights. H

16 4 CYLINDER INDIAN CYCLE, 9 1/4", made from the late 1920s into the 1930s. This motorcycle could also be purchased with a sport rider instead of a policeman. It came with nickeled spoke wheels and 4 cylinder engine, an exhaust clicker, and black rubber tires. It could be ordered in red, green, or yellow. E

A page from the 1932 Hubley catalog showing the Indian Side Car Motorcycle No. 778 with two sport figures.

11 2 CYLINDER HARLEY-DAVIDSON PARCEL POST CYCLE, 9 1/2", made from the late 1920s until about 1933. It was only available in olive and came with an exhaust clicker, separate rider, and a door on the side car. G

A page from the 1932 Hubley catalog showing the Harley-Davidson Side Car Motorcycle No. 36 with two sport figures.

309 FLOWER VAN CYCLE, 4 1/4", part of the Hubley midget line. The Flower cycles were made in six sizes and all are scarce. E

16 4 CYLINDER INDIAN CYCLE, 9 1/4". This toy has a clicker, a nickel plated engine, and a separate rider and cast aluminum handlebars. It was offered in yellow, red, and green and was made from 1929 through 1941. It came with a cop or a sports rider, but from 1934 on it was only available in red with a cop rider. E

37 4 CYLINDER INDIAN FLOWER VAN, 10 3/4", made for only a couple of years starting in 1931. This toy is arguably considered the most desirable of all cast iron automotive toys from the standpoints of design, subject, and scarcity. Only a handful are known to exist. K

Detail.

349 INDIAN TRAFFIC CAR, 3 1/4", with a cast-in driver and nickeled wheels. This toy was also made in two larger sizes as shown. It was introduced in 1931 and was discontinued in 1934. C

46-F 2 CYLINDER SIDECAR MOTORCYCLE, 3 1/2", made from 1934 to 1941. It came with a Hubley decal (few Hubley toys possess a decal), a cop rider, and is called the generic version. It is scarcer than the Indian or Harley sidecar cycles. F

27 INDIAN CRASH CAR, 11 1/2". It came with 3 wooden canisters, a hose reel, and fire-axes. It first appears in the 1931 catalog supplement and was produced through 1941. H

INDIAN ARMORED CAR, 8 3/4", 1928 to about 1933. This toy has a sidecar rider and a removable shield. F

343 INDIAN TRAFFIC CAR, 4 1/2", made from 1931 until about 1934. C

38 2 CYLINDER INDIAN TRAFFIC CAR CYCLE, 8 3/4", 1930s. Four other sizes were manufactured during the 1930s: 3 5/8", 4 3/4", 6 1/2", and 12". This next to largest traffic car came with nickel plated cast iron wheels or stamped spoked wheels with white rubber tires. E

615 INDIAN TRAFFIC CAR, 6 1/4", made from 1931 until about 1934. D

39 2 CYLINDER INDIAN CRASH CAR CYCLE, 9 3/4", 1930s. Three other crash car cycles were made during the 1930s in 4 3/4", 6 3/4", and 11 1/2". This one came with two wood containers and a fire hose on a reel. G

18 POPEYE PATROL, 8 3/4", made from 1938 through 1940. This highly desirable toy has a removable Popeye figure with arms that move at the shoulders. This toy was reproduced in 1982 and the reproduction cycle and rider were very well done and are difficult for a novice collector to tell from an original. H

622 POPEYE SPINACH DELIVERY CYCLE, 5 1/2". Around 1938 to 1940. Popeye is removable. F

TRUCKS

313 AUTO DRAY, 4", made from the teens into the mid 1920s. A

737 AUTO EXPRESS WITH ROOF, 9 1/4". The roof is
light gauge steel as is the floor. This toy was made prior to
the 1920s until about 1930. It comes with a black driver. F

783 AUTO STAKE TRUCK, 17". This toy is also called the 5 TON TRUCK. It was
probably made well before 1920 and production of it carried through until around
1929. It has a separate tailgate, a steel floor, and a large separate driver. F

738 AUTO EXPRESS, 9 1/4". This toy was probably made prior to 1920 and until about the mid 1920s. It has a steel floor and a black driver. F

722 COAL TRUCK, 9 1/2", made prior to 1920 and through 1932. Other sizes were also made. F

739 AUTO DRAY, 10 1/4", made during the 1920s. A smaller size of this toy was also available. F

741 AUTO TRUCK, 10", shown in the 1928 catalog as also being available in 8 3/4" and 6 3/4". This toy was made during the 1920s. F

679 MERCHANT'S DELIVERY TRUCK, 6", made only during the 1920s and in two sizes, 6" and 7 3/8". D

308 DELIVERY VAN, 4 3/4", made during the 1930s but generally found with "Hubley" in script on the side panel. C

750 TRUK-MIXER, 7 3/4", made for several years starting in 1932. Its drum turns as the toy is rolled on the floor. This is considered a scarce and desirable toy. H

321 BABY OUTBOARD MOTOR BOAT, 4 1/4", 1932, and 308 DELIVERY VAN, 4 3/4", 1932 with Hubley in raised letters on the side. Both toys can be found in the 1932 Hubley catalog as part of their "midget line." B; C

617 RAILWAY EXPRESS TRUCK, 5", also produced in 4" and 6 1/2" sizes, produced from 1932 to about 1935. C

747 MACK GAS TRUCK, 11", mid 1920s until about 1930. This is a scarce truck. It was also made in a 9" size and several smaller sizes. It came with a nickeled driver. G

746 MACK DUMP TRUCK, 11", 1920s until 1941. This truck was made in 6 sizes. It has a spring-operated bed operated by a lever. F

742 MACK GAS TRUCK, 9", introduced in the 1920s. This toy was dropped from the line around 1930. Other smaller sizes were produced until the mid 1930s. F

746 MACK DUMP TRUCK, 11", 1920s-1941. This is the early version of a truck made from the 1920s until the war years. It came with a nickeled driver. F

613 MACK DUMP TRUCK, 5 1/4". From the late 1920s, Mack Dump Trucks were made in a half dozen lengths, but like some of their other toys, Hubley would offer certain sizes one year and other sizes the next year. By the late 1930s, the company only offered the 11" size. D

334 MACK AUTO TRUCK, 3 1/2", made from 1930 to around 1933. In the 1932 catalog it is simply called a Dray. B

637 MACK STAKE TRUCK, 5 3/4". In the late 1920s, this toy was available in 9", 6 3/4", 5 3/4", and 4 1/2", but by 1934 it was only made in the two smaller sizes. C

315 MACK AUTO TRUCK, 4 1/4". It was made from the late 1920s until about 1935 in five sizes ranging from 8 1/2", 6 3/4", 5 1/2", 4 1/4", and 3 1/2". C

733 MACK DUMP TRUCK, 8 1/2", early 1930s. This truck was made only briefly during the early 1930s. It has a spring-operated dump like the larger versions. E

611 STUDEBAKER DUMP TRUCK with nickel plated grill, 7", made from 1934-1940. D

681 DUMP TRUCK, 6 3/4", 1932-1936. Move the
lever and a spring causes the bed to dump. D

743 MACK DUMP TRUCK, 8 3/4", late 1920s to about 1935.
This Mack Dump Truck has a spring-operated dump bed.
Moving the lever next to the driver causes the bed to dump. E

320 DUMP TRUCK, 4", part of the Hubley midget line in the late 1930s. C

665 WRECKER with DETACHABLE BODY, 6 3/4". When introduced in 1933 this and the stake truck were tutone. A year or so later they were available in a single color. This Wrecker has silver paint added to the side of bed and boom by some creative child. C

654 BORDEN'S MILK TRUCK, 6", early 1930s for a couple of years. D

42 BORDEN'S MILK TRUCK, 7 3/4", 1930s. Nickeled grill, driver, and rear door. This size was made during the first half of the 1930s and also has been found with a decal instead of the name "Borden's" in raised letters. This truck is a nice model of the DIVCO (Detroit Industrial Vehicle Company) trucks that were used for deliveries during the 1930s. H

314 MILK DELIVERY TRUCK, 3 3/4", available during the 1930s. B

40 BELL TELEPHONE TRUCK, 10", 1930s-1941. Came with same equipment as No. 41 except the auger. F

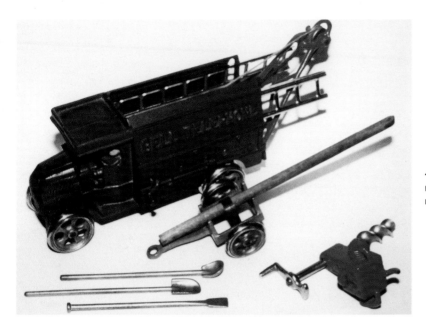

41 BELL TELEPHONE TRUCK, 10". This version has nickel plated cast iron wheels instead of the more common white rubber tires on red-painted wood hubs. G

638 BELL TELEPHONE TRUCK, 5 1/4", 1930s. These telephone trucks were one of Hubley's largest sellers and were available throughout the 1930s in 6 sizes ranging from 3" to 10". C

354 BELL TELEPHONE TRUCK, 3", 1932-1935. This is the smallest of the Hubley Mack Bell Telephone Trucks. Hubley made thousands of Telephone Trucks but today finding this size can be a challenge. C

41 BELL TELEPHONE TRUCK, 10". This is the largest of the five sizes introduced in 1931. By the late 1930s the 10" size was the only one being made. A sixth size was added during the mid 1930s for a couple of years. The largest was offered in red for a brief period. The toy pictured has all the original equipment including a pull cord and a coil of rope on the roof. F

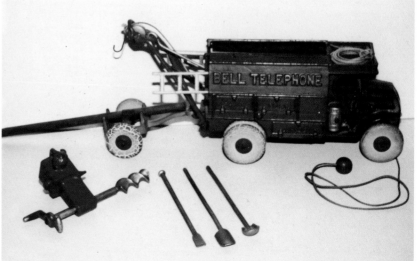

663 STAKE TRUCK with DETACHABLE BODY, 6 1/2", introduced in 1933 as part of a series of cars and trucks from 1933-1935. C

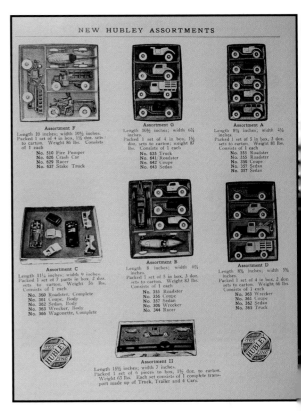

Boxed sets shown in the 1933 catalog.

680 TRANSPORT TRUCK, 10", 1938-1941. This came equipped with four 3 1/2" autos. In this case a Coupe, a Convertible, and two Sedans. E

776 NUCAR TRANSPORT, 16", Introduced in 1934 and continued through 1941. This toy came with a car, truck, racer, and Nite Coach Bus. It looks much better equipped with the four vehicles as shown. In 1933 Hubley did offer a boxed assortment of autos similar to these but these are actually Kilgore. F

306 "SERVICE CAR" WRECKER, 4 3/4", 1930. Earlier than the other two small wreckers pictured, this depicts the typical conversion of an auto into a wrecker done by many small repair shops. B

*WRECKER, 4 1/2", 1934-1935. It came with separate chassis and nickeled grill. Series also had a pick-up truck. C

TWO WRECKERS, 306, 5" and 347, 3 3/4".
Both early 1930s. Wreckers were part of the
popular Hubley "midget line," and continued
to be made throughout the early 1930s. B

357 Wrecker, 5 1/2", 1936-1939, with white rubber tires
and painted red centers and a nickel plated boom. B

FIRE ENGINES

529 HOOK AND LADDER TRUCK, 13 1/2", 1941. E

445 AUTO CHEMICAL TRUCK, 12 1/4", 1920s. This toy was made
during the 1920s. Several other sizes were made, one larger and
two smaller. This version has a nickel plated chemical tank, a hose
reel that is removable, four loose ladder supports, and a separate
driver. It came with two wooden ladders. The front axle pivots. I

552 AUTO FIRE ENGINE, 14", made during the 1920s to resemble real pumpers with the motorized Christie front end. This is known by collectors as a Hubley transitional pumper in that it fills the gap between the transition from horse drawn to motorized fire equipment. I

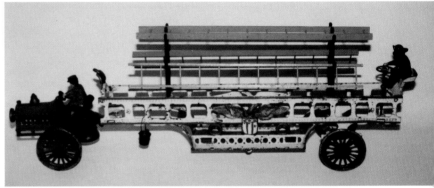

555 AUTO HOOK and LADDER, 29", 1920s. A smaller version was also made. This is known as a transitional fire truck. It was made like the real ones, which had a motorized Christie front end that was coupled to the horse-drawn back end, thus saving the need to buy the entire hook and ladder unit.

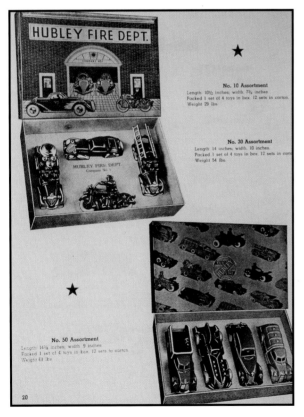

1936 catalog showing two boxed sets.

Hubley FIRE DEPART-MENT SET, no. 10, from the late 1930s.

530 AHRENS-FOX PUMPER, 11 1/2", 1932-1941. It came with a nickel plated pump at the front, two nickeled ladders, and a nickeled driver. This is certainly one of the nicest cast iron fire engines ever made. It has great lines and lots of detail. Hubley made five smaller versions: 9 1/4", 7", 6 3/4", 4 1/2", and 3 5/8". G

518 FIRE ENGINE, 8 1/2", 1934-1940. Nickel plated fireman, grill and boiler top. D

Detail of AHRENS-FOX PUMPER ENGINE.

519, FIRE LADDER TRUCK, 9 1/2", 1934-1940. With nickel plated firemen and grill. The ladders were plated but some small "fireman" must have thought that they looked better painted brown. D

313 AHRENS-FOX PUMPER, 4 1/2", made from about 1932-1934. C

510 AHRENS-FOX PUMPER, 7 1/2", made from about 1932 to 1934. E

CONSTRUCTION EQUIPMENT

325 STEAM SHOVEL, 4 1/2", late 1920s to about 1933. B

668 MONARCH BULLDOZER, 5 1/2", 1932-1933. As this bulldozer moves, a cam makes the body rock. The name "Hubley" is cast in raised letters underneath the body. E

736 PANAMA STEAM SHOVEL, 9", 10" when shovel is extended. This toy was made during the 1920s and production continued into the 1930s. F

301 WONDER CEMENT MIXER, 3 1/2", available during the 1930s. B

735 HUBER STEAM DRIVEN ROAD ROLLER, 8", 1928-1941. Children loved to play with realistic toys that simulated adult work. Construction and building vehicles have always been some of the most popular toys for young boys. This road roller was a fairly common toy and remained a popular seller from 1928-1941. This version is painted olive with gold striping. Another version was painted orange with black striping. D

A page from the 1932 catalog

727 FORDSON TRACTOR WITH SHOVEL, 9 1/4", 1930s.
Nickel plated driver and shovel. Some shovels are painted silver.
Also came with black rubber tires with painted centers. G

31 ELGIN STREET SWEEPER, 8 1/2", early 1930s. This very complex toy actually works with a brush that sweeps into a dumping compartment. It also has a hose and coupling for taking on water from a hydrant. Hubley gained a reputation for making toys that were usually more complex than those of other cast iron toy makers. This toy was only made for a few years during the early 1930s. I

Details of Sweeper.

711 HUBER DIESEL ROAD ROLLER with vertical tank, 15", 1928. This toy is believed to have been made for just a year before it was redesigned with many detail changes plus a horizontal nickel plated tank and scarifier. This toy was a Hubley "exclusive right toy" and the company probably had to change the toy when Huber changed the design of the real road roller. The second version continued to be manufactured from 1929-1933. H

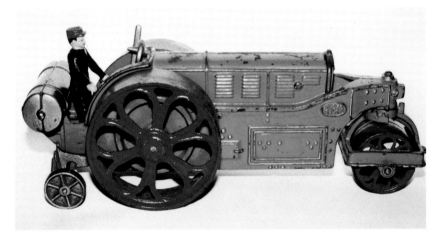

711 HUBER DIESEL ROAD ROLLER with horizontal tank, 15", 1929-1933. G

684 ALLIS-CHALMERS FARM TRACTOR, 7", 1939-1941.
Hubley frequently got the rights to produce accurate replicas
of well-known brand names. This toy is an example. The
driver seat and control levers are separate castings. D

334 TRACTOR, 3 3/4", late 1930s. Another product in the Hubley Midget Line. Most of these tractors had wooden wheels like this one. A

751 PANAMA STEAM SHOVEL TRUCK, 12 3/4", 1931 to about 1937. This early version of the toy came in this color combination and had cast iron wheels. While this gray and red variety was made for a longer period than the green and red ones, fewer turn up. G

346 MACK SHOVEL TRUCK, 4 1/4", early 1930s. This toy looks like the early PANAMA STEAM SHOVEL TRUCK. C

656 MACK GENERAL SHOVEL TRUCK, 8 1/2", 1930s. This toy came in four sizes ranging in size from 4 1/4" to 10". Early ones in this size were red and gray. Later they came in red and green, which is the most common color variation. D

751 PANAMA STEAM SHOVEL TRUCK, 12 3/4", 1931 through 1939. It was painted gray and red for the first six or so years and then green and red. The early versions had nickel plated cast iron wheels. F

AIRPLANES

319 AIRFORD, 4", 1929. This single engine airplane has two passengers and was made for several years starting in 1929. B

630 "LINDY" AIRPLANE, 6", 1932. Nickel plated propeller and wheels. This is a very hard size to find. Usually Hubley did not mark its toys but this toy has the name Hubley marked in raised letters under the wing. D

4 "BREMEN" AIRPLANE, 7 1/4", late 1920s. The Bremen made the first successful westward flight across the Atlantic in the late 1920s. Three flyers are visible in the windows. This toy was also made in a larger size but since it was only manufactured for a few years, it is now hard to find in either size. F

Amelia Earhart was a popular aviation heroine of the 1920s. In 1928 Earhart became the first woman passenger to cross the Atlantic Ocean by air. In 1932 she set another record when she became the first woman to fly across the Atlantic alone. In 1937 she tried to become the first woman to fly around the world. Her plane disappeared over the Pacific Ocean and her disappearance remains a mystery today.

15 "FRIENDSHIP" AIRPLANE, 11", 1929. All three propellers turn when rolled along. It was modeled after Amelia Earhart's plane. It was only made for several years starting in the year 1929. It has the word "Fokker" in raised letters on the fuselage. I

Charles Lindbergh started his aviation career as a mail pilot for the U.S. Post office. In 1919 American industrialist Raymond Orteig offered a prize of $25,000 to the first man to fly solo across the Atlantic. Lindbergh was determined to win that prize and eight years later he succeeded, flying a single-engine plane, *Spirit of St. Louis*, across the Atlantic Ocean and arriving outside of Paris on May 21, 1927.

Two years later Lindbergh married Anne Morrow who was herself a licensed pilot. In 1930 the two set a new international flight record, and in 1931 they flew to the Orient as "ambassadors of good will." The couple often flew together and pioneered new routes for American airlines to fly to Europe, Asia, and Latin America. Hubley and Dent both made many airplanes with the name "Lindy" in raised letters on the wings.

"The popularity of this famous aviator is shared by the handsome airplane toy that bears the name made illustrious by a daring flight," says the 1929 Hubley catalog.

*LOCKHEED SIRIUS, 8 1/2", early 1930s. Aluminum body with cast iron propeller and engine. This was Charles and Anne Morrow Lindbergh's private aircraft. The Hubley toy no. 379 has "Lindy" on one wing and NR-211 on the other wing. The toy shown here is unusual because it is made of aluminum, has a cast iron propeller and engine, and doesn't have markings on the wings. It is not known when this version was produced. The all cast iron version was made for just a few years in the early 1930s and is quite scarce. I

302 DO-X DORNIER SEAPLANE, 4 3/4", 1930-1936. This toy was first introduced in 1930 and was manufactured in four sizes. This one is the next to the smallest. Today the largest size is very difficult to find. The name Hubley is found inside the fuselage. C

322 "LINDY" AIRPLANE, 3 3/4", 1932. Nickel plated wheels and propeller. Usually Hubley did not mark its toys but this toy has the name Hubley marked in raised letters under the wing. B

304 GIROPLANE, 4 1/2", 1930-1936. Stamped and plated rotor and nickel plated engine, propeller, and wheels. The name Hubley is found under the wing. C

From a page in the 1929 Hubley catalog center fold-out.

7 "LINDY" AIRPLANE, 11 1/4", 1928-1933. It has white rubber tires and wooden hubs. The propeller turns as the toy is rolled along. It also has a clicker. The toy generally has a "Spirit of St. Louis" decal just behind the engine. Hubley made many sizes of this plane for about six years from 1928 to 1933. F

*LINDY GLIDER, 6 1/2". This toy is a 1980s reproduction of a toy that was made by Hubley in the 1930s. C

*LINDY GLIDER, 10". This toy is a 1980s reproduction of a toy that was made by Hubley in the 1930s. This large size has a removable pilot. D

398 TRANSATLANTIC TRANSPORT (TAT) 4 1/4". Has nickeled wings and a cast iron propeller. B

305 SINGLE-ENGINE PLANE, 3 1/2", late 1930s. Nickel plated wings and propeller. The name "Hubley" is cast under the wings. A

172

303 SINGLE ENGINE PLANE, 4 1/2", late 1930s. Nickel plated wings and propeller, white rubber tires. This plane was produced in several sizes. B

378 AIRLINER, 4 1/4", late 1930s. Cast iron propellers, white rubber tires. B

305 SINGLE ENGINE PLANE, 3 1/2" and 316 DC-3, 3". Both circa late 1930s, with cast iron propellers and white rubber tires. A

CAST IRON ART ITEMS

Hubley produced a line of cast iron art goods during the 1930s consisting of door knockers, paper weights, etc. Popeye, Olive Oyl, and Wimpy are a sample of a few of these beautifully painted products that are the right size to be perfect 'go-withs' for cast iron vehicles. They are about 3 inches tall.

Popeye and Olive Oyl were two popular comic characters of the 1930s and 1940s. First created by Elsie C. Segar for King Features in 1929, the sailor boy with bulging biceps claimed that he got his strength from eating his spinach. Soon parents were promoting spinach as a food for their children to eat to grow big and strong.

Popeye, Olive Oyl, and Wimpy, 3" h., 1930s. A set of three is in the D range.

4. KENTON

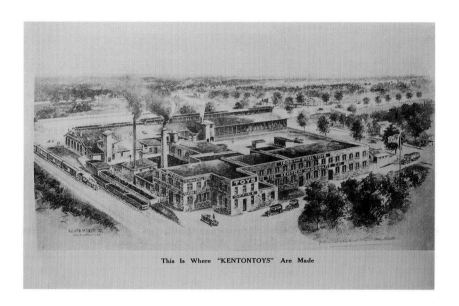

This Is Where "KENTONTOYS" Are Made

Kenton Toys were first produced by the Kenton Hardware Company in Kenton, Ohio, in the 1890s. Originally called the Kenton Lock Manufacturing Company, the company produced toys until 1952 when production ceased.

Lewis Sharps Bixler was appointed general manager of Kenton in 1909 and under his leadership the company thrived. Bixler came from a toy background. From 1889 through 1899 he had worked for his uncle's foundry, William Shimer and Son, a cast iron toy manufacturing company in Freemansburg, a small village between Bethlehem and Easton, Pennsylvania.

The next year Bixler and C.A. Jones opened their own company, Jones & Bixler, but in 1901 that company closed and merged with the larger conglomerate the National Toy Novelty Company, which acquired an interest in Kenton. In 1909 Bixler moved to Kenton.

Some of the toys in the earliest Kenton catalogs—horse-drawn vehicles such as Hansom Cabs, spider phaetons, and cabriolets; the early touring cars; and the 1901 large fire department series—resemble earlier Jones & Bixler models.

AUTOMOBILE, 9 1/2". This toy does not appear in available catalogs. It is similar to the 504 in the Jones & Bixler and Kenton catalogs, except that those do not have a roof. The toy is quite scarce and probably was made prior to 1904 for a couple of years. It has a tiller, a driver, and a passenger. G

507 TOURIST CAR, 9 1/2", early 1900s. It was first made by Jones & Bixler and is in their 1908 catalog but without front doors. By 1911 the car is shown in the Kenton catalog with the same 507 number. This toy was not continued when toy production resumed after World War I. It has a separate driver and passenger. F

505 AUTOMOBILE, 9 1/2", early 1900s. First made by Jones & Bixler and later by Kenton. Kenton retained the Jones & Bixler number but discontinued this car after World War I. It came with a separate driver and passenger. F

492 TOURING CAR, 11 1/2". This toy was made from 1915 to about 1924. It was also made as a 9 1/2" version. It came with a driver and lady passenger who wore a scarf around her neck . F

The New Model Coupe and Sedan each came with a separate driver. The two largest sizes also had separate spare tires.

94 COUPE, 5 1/4", 1920-1927. Came with a separate driver. C

695 NEW MODEL COUPE, 6 1/2", early 1920s-1929. Came with a separate driver and spare wheel. D

696 NEW MODEL COUPE, 8", 1923 to about 1926. Has separate driver. F

697 NEW MODEL COUPE, 9 3/4", 1923 to about
1926. Has separate driver and steering wheel. G

494 SEDAN, 5 3/4", 1920-1927.
Came with a separate driver.

497 YELLOW TAXI, 9 3/4", 1923-1929. Has separate driver and steering wheel. G

495 SEDAN, 6 1/2", 1923-1929. Has separate driver. D

497 SEDAN, 9 3/4", 1923-1929. Has separate driver and steering wheel. F

Kenton assembled some of their smaller toys complete with axles and wheels and then dipped them to apply the main color coat. They then decorated them by applying silver to the tires and headlights and perhaps gold for highlights and sometimes black on the fenders and roofs. Toys that some believe to have been repainted because their axles are painted may actually be original factory finishes. The black paint that Kenton used did not always dry or cure properly, and is known to have severely crazed and migrated into small patches. This usually occurred with toys that had been stored in hot attics over a period of time.

350 COUPE, 8 1/4", introduced around 1927 through 1929. The toy has a separate driver and spare tire. G

450 SEDAN, 8", 1927 through 1929. This toy has a separately cast chassis which gives it greater detail. G

352 COUPE, 10", about 1927 through 1929. The toy has a separate driver and spare tire that says "STOP 1928." This version has a series of horizontal louvers on the hood sides. The toy is pictured in the catalogs with vertical louvers. H

SEDAN

New principle of chassis cast separate in one piece. Extra tire with Red and Green lights showing at back.

No. 450—Painted and decorated.   Length 8¼ inches.   1 in a box.   3 dozen in a case.   Weight of case 115 lbs.

No. 452—Painted and decorated.   Length 10¼ inches.   1 in a box.   3 dozen in a case.   Weight of case 180 lbs.

No. 454—Painted and decorated.   Length 12½ inches.   1 dozen in a case.   Weight of case 135 lbs.

COUPE

No. 350—Painted and decorated.   Length 8¼ inches.   1 in a box.   3 dozen in a case.   Weight of case 110 lbs.

No. 352—Painted and decorated.   Length 10 inches.   1 in a box.   3 dozen in a case.   Weight of case 190 lbs.

A page from the 1927 Kenton catalog.

516 AUTO BUS, 8 1/4", 1914-1923.
Came with a separate driver. G

519 CITY BUS, 6 3/4", 1928-1941.
Came with a clamped-in driver. E

518 AUTO BUS, 6 1/4", 1914-1923. Came with a
separate driver. The passengers were made by Kenton
but probably were only used in their later buses. F

519 CITY BUS, 6 3/4", 1928-1941. Came with a clamped-in driver and passengers. E

522 CITY BUS, 10", 1928-1941. Came with a clamped-in driver and passengers. E

523 CITY BUS, 11 1/2", 1928-1941. Came with a clamped-in driver and passengers. F

156 PICKWICK NITE COACH, 11", 1930-1933. These buses were used primarily along Californian highways for several years during the late 1920s and early 1930s. They had sleeping compartments. Kenton made five versions of this bus. The one pictured is the next to the largest. All the larger sizes are scarce. This toy came with a clamped-in driver, separate bumper, and spare tire. G

182

A page from the *Saturday Evening Post*.

*TROLLEY, 8 1/2". We surmise that Kenton made this trolley. D

*TROLLEY, 12 1/4". Attributed to Kenton but not found in any of the catalogs. E

An original KENTON CONCRETE MIXER BOX.

899 SIGHT SEEING AUTO, 10 1/2". Made from about 1910 to mid 1920s. It was also made with "Seeing New York" on the side. Both toys are very desirable and scarce autos and have five comic character figures from the early funnies. These popular contemporary comic strip characters are Mama Katzenjammer, Happy Hooligan, Gloomy Gus, and the Captain. H

Page from the Kent catalog.

THE KENTON HARDWARE CO., KENTON, OHIO   53

Auto Cab

No. 510½—Painted and Decorated. 4 inches long. 12 in a box. 24 dozen in a case. Weight per case, 225 lbs.

No. 511 —Painted and Decorated. 5 inches long. 12 in a box. 12 dozen in a case. Weight per case, 160 lbs.

No. 512 —Painted and Decorated. 6 inches long. 3 in a box. 6 dozen in a case. Weight per case, 150 lbs.

No. 514 —Painted and Decorated. 8 inches long. 1 in a box. 3 dozen in a case. Weight per case, 130 lbs.

Sight Seeing Auto Car

No. 899   Painted. Length, 10½ inches. 1 in a box. 2 dozen in a case. Weight per case, 160 lbs.

TRUCKS

188 AUTO CONTRACTOR'S WAGON, 8", 1914 to 1931. This toy has three lever actuated dumping buckets, a separate driver, and steering wheel. E

1703 AUTO AMBULANCE, 7 1/4", 1911 to the mid 1920s. Has a separate driver and was also available nickel plated. E

184 AUTO COAL WAGON, 7 1/2", 1914 to mid 1930s. This toy has a dumping bed, a separate driver, steering wheel (which is rarely found with the toy), and is numbered "848" on the left side. D

1603 AUTO AMBULANCE, 5 1/2", 1911 to mid 1920s. Has a separate nickeled driver. (Toy also came nickel plated.) E

556 TANK TRUCK, 9 3/4", introduced around 1926
and made until 1931. Has a separate driver. F

276 WRECK CAR, 9 3/4", introduced in 1924 and discontinued by 1928. This toy has a working wrecker winch, and a
separate driver. It was made in a slightly smaller size. The
toy pictured here was from the Kenton Sample Room. G

560 CITY SERVICE TRUCK, 10 1/4", introduced in 1924 and discontinued by 1932. This truck has a separate driver. The toy pictured here
was from the Kenton Sample Room and has a 1924 Sample tag. H

248 SPRINKLER TRUCK, 7", 1927 to the mid 1930s. Has separate driver. D

557 MACK TANK TRUCK, 11 1/4", 1925-1929. This very colorful and impressive truck has a separate driver. The tank body is bolted onto the chassis. This toy is very scarce and finding one in this fine condition is a real treat and very difficult. H

562R DUMP TRUCK, 8 1/4", 1932-1935. Made with the driver clamped in when the body halves were riveted together, which keeps the driver from falling out. D

530 MACK LIFT DUMP TRUCK, 11 1/4",
mid 1920s to 1930s. Turn the crank and the
dump bed lifts. Has a separate driver. F

532 MACK LIFT DUMP TRUCK,
14 3/4", mid 1920s to mid 1930s.
Turn the crank and the dump bed
lifts. Has a separate driver. Pictured
towing #650 JAEGER CEMENT
MIXER. G

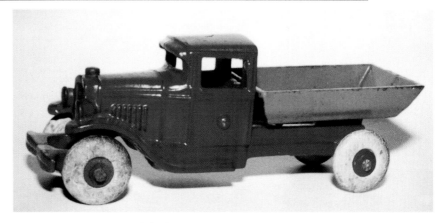

529R DUMP TRUCK,
6 1/4", 1932-1935. D

406 OVERLAND CIRCUS HIPPOPOTAMUS CAGE
TRUCK , 9", made for a couple of years in the mid
1920s. The catalog also shows a smaller 8" cage and
two sizes of calliope trucks. This toy has a separate
driver, a hippopotamus, and a fold-down tail gate. G

*SPEED TRUCK 15 3/4", not known when produced. This toy has a separate driver, a fold-down tail gate, and a nickel-plated bumper. It came in three smaller sizes that were made from the mid 1920s to about the 1930s. This large size is very scarce. I

3130R COAL TRUCK, 10 1/2", 1932-1935. Came with a clamped-in driver who is so short that he can't see out the windshield. F

363 ICE TRUCK, 10", 1927-1931. This open cab Ice Truck has a separate driver. It is the largest of three sizes. F

655R JAEGER DRUM TYPE CONCRETE MIXER TRUCK, 7", 1932-1940. Has a nickel plated drum that revolves as the toy is rolled on the floor. F

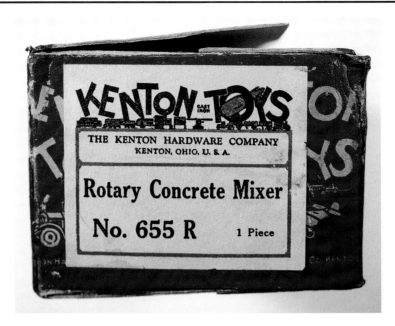

At some point in the 1930s Kenton stopped
using the R suffix to denote rubber tires.

*COAL TRUCK, 7 3/4", 1936-1938. The toy is
equipped with a nickel plated grill/bumper. E

657R JAEGER DRUM TYPE CONCRETE MIXER TRUCK, 9 1/4", 1932-
1940. This toy has a clamped-in driver and a nickel plated revolving drum.
In 1950 a slightly modified version of this toy was introduced with black
rubber wheels and painted red. It isn't shown in the 1951 catalog. G

*ICE TRUCK, 7 1/4", 1936-1938. This toy has a separate nickel plated grill/bumper. D

552R STANDARD OIL TRUCK, 12 3/4", 1933. The driver is clamped-in and there is a separate nickel plated bumper. The truck is unusual in that it is a tractor/trailer. This scarce toy was apparently only made for one year. It also came in a 9 1/2" Texaco version. H

1008 GAS TRUCK, 4 1/4", 1936-1938. This cute toy has a separate chassis and a nickel plated grill. C

FIRE ENGINES

1977 AUTO HOSE WAGON, 8 1/4", 1911 until the mid 1920s. This toy has a separate driver, separate steering wheel and rack with lanterns cast-in, a hose, and a fireman. F

2937 HOOK AND LADDER TRUCK, 20 1/2", 1928-1941. This truck has a separate driver, a fireman, a nickel plated bumper, three nickeled ladder racks, and three ladders. The truck also has a bell. This toy was made in many sizes during the 1930s. E

1827 AUTO POLICE PATROL, 9", 1911 until the mid 1920s. This toy has a driver, a prisoner, and two policemen. It also has a separate steering wheel. F

2974 HOSE AND LADDER TRUCK, 9", 1928-1932. This toy has a separate driver, two nickel plated hose racks, a hose, and two metal ladders. D

CONSTRUCTION EQUIPMENT

3116 POWER SHOVEL, 6 3/4",
1931-1932. This toy is the largest
of three sizes. It has a nickel
plated shovel and wheels. D

2805 TRACTOR, 5 1/4", 1928-1931.
This toy has nickel plated wheels. It
was made for a year or two in four
sizes. It has a sample room tag. D

2805 1/2 TRACTOR, 6", 1930 through the mid
1930s. This has a separate nickel plated driver
and nickel plated wheels. It was made for a
year or two in four different sizes. D

3110 GALION MASTER ROAD ROLLER, 6 3/4", 1931-1950. This toy was produced in the 1930s as #3110. It was reintroduced in 1950 as #152. Several other sizes were made over the twenty-year period. D

507 BUCKEYE DITCHER, 9", 1931-1950. E

508 BUCKEYE DITCHER, 13 3/4", 1930-1941. Two cranks are provided to operate the buckets and raise and lower the boom. F

510 FAIRFIELD LOADER, 9 3/4", 1932.
Made for only one year, this is a scarce
toy. It was also made in a larger size. G

500 HORIZONTAL ENGINE, 8", 1930-
1933. This engine, when hand cranked,
operates in a realistic manner. It was also
made in a larger size. They are difficult
to find complete. F

652 JAEGER CONCRETE
MIXER, 7", 1930-1941. E

650 JAEGER CONCRETE MIXER, 6 3/4", 1930-1950. This common toy is very well made and nicely detailed. The lift bucket and hopper are made of aluminum. E

3150 MORGAN CRANE, 16" x 12 1/4" x 12". This toy was made during the early 1930s and could actually be operated like a real one. H

AIRPLANES

672 AIR MAIL AIRPLANE, 8 3/4", 1930 through the mid 1930s. F

684 LOS ANGELES DIRI-GIBLE, 11 1/4", 1930 through the mid 1930s. F

680 PONY BLIMP, 5 3/4", 1930 through the mid 1930s. D

5. KILGORE "Toys That Last"

The Kilgore Manufacturing Company was founded in the 1920s in Westerville, Ohio, and produced a line of small toys such as a tailless kite called the E-Z-FLY kite and cast iron cap guns, cannons, and toy paper caps. In 1925 the company bought the George D. Wanner Company of Dayton, Ohio, the largest manufacturer of kites in the United States. In 1928 the company joined with the Andes Foundry Company and the Federal Toy Company to form the American Toy Company and began to produce cast iron trucks, cars, and fire engines. Some of its most popular products were a series of small boxed sets of toys that retailed for fifty cents. Kilgore survived the Depression but later decided to concentrate only on producing toy cap pistols and toy paper caps. In 1944 the company ceased production.

AUTOMOBILES

T-78 SPORT ROADSTER, 8", circa 1920s. Like the smaller version, this toy has an opening rumble seat, a separate nickeled driver, and is marked "Kilgore." E

T-76 SPORT ROADSTER, 4 1/4", probably made in the mid 1920s. This toy has a folding rumble seat, a separate driver, and is marked "Kilgore." It is hard to find this little car especially with the driver intact. C

T-60 COUPE, 6 1/4", 1920s. This toy, marked "Kilgore," has a nickel plated man and a woman, which are both mounted on a short spring so that they "jiggle" when the toy is moved. This toy is hard to find complete with its passengers. A variation of this toy was offered in 1926 with a trunk lid that opened. D

T-22 FORD SEDAN, 3 1/4"; and T-23 FORD ROADSTER, 3 1/4". These two toys represent the Model A Ford introduced in late 1927. They were made from 1928 through 1932. The Roadster is almost always missing the nickeled driver. The Sedan is marked "Kilgore," but the Roadster is unmarked. Both A

312 SEDAN, 6 3/4", part of the Graham series, 1933. F

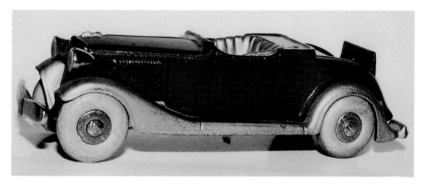

310 ROADSTER, 6 3/4", 1933. This toy was introduced in 1933 and is modeled after a Graham. It has a separate body, chassis seat, and nickeled grill. Two longitudinal wires connect the body and chassis together and lock the axles in place. Kilgore used this unique form of construction starting in 1933 on some of their products. The Graham series was made in two sizes and there were three cars and three trucks in each size. The 6 3/4" Roadster is very scarce. It is not known how long Kilgore continued to make these toys. G

311 COUPE, 6 3/4", 1933. This toy is part of the Graham series. Several of these toys have been found nickel plated like this. Perhaps they were made as salesmen's samples or for some special event. F

22 COUPE, 4". This toy is part of the Graham series and was introduced in 1933. It was assembled like the 6 3/4" version with two longitudinal wires. B

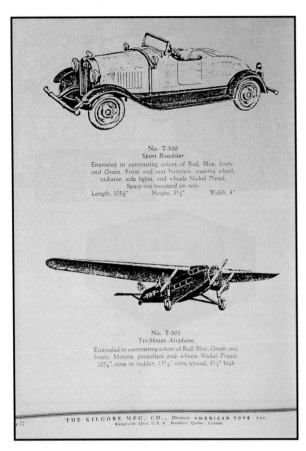

Page from the 1931 KILGORE catalog
showing two desirable large cast iron toys.

T-500 SPORT ROADSTER, 10 1/2", from 1930 to about 1932. This toy, which is marked "Kilgore" on the chassis, has ten separate nickel plated parts and is believed to be modeled after the Stutz Roadster. The plated parts were made of cast iron or an alloy (probably to reduce breakage). Original toys have been found with some parts made of iron and others of the alloy material. G

*ROADSTER, 3 1/2"; SEDAN, 3 1/2". Both circa 1933. It is not known when production ceased. Both B

*COUPE, 3 1/2", around 1933. This little auto is put together with two wires, which hold the body to the chassis and contain the axles. Three cars and a handful of trucks comprise this series that was introduced around 1933. It is not known when production of these plump little vehicles ceased. B

*MOTORCYCLE, 5 3/4", circa 1930s. This motorcycle came with rubber tires and nickel plated wheels. D

T-379 MOTORCYCLE WITH SIDE CAR, 5", circa 1931. D

TRUCKS

A group of seven Kilgore cars and trucks. Trucks each 3 1/2". B

*EXPRESS TRUCK, 3 1/2", 1933. This truck is part of the 3 1/2" series of wired construction cars and trucks produced from about 1933. B

T-6 DELIVERY TRUCK, 3 1/4", 1920s and early 1930s. This truck was found in several boxed sets as well as being sold separately. B

*WRECKER, 3 3/4", mid 1930s, wired construction. B

*DUMP TRUCK, 6", wired construction made during the mid 1930s. D

*PICK UP TRUCK, 3 3/4", mid 1930s, wired construction. B

26 EXPRESS TRUCK, 4", 1933, wired construction. This truck is part of the nickeled grill, 4" series introduced by the company in 1933. B

T-503 AIRPORT TENDER GAS TRUCK, 12 3/4", 1931-1932. This aviation gas truck was one of three large trucks made by Kilgore from 1931 through 1932. The others were a wrecker and a low boy tractor trailer. All are desirable and hard to find toys. G

27 WRECKER, 4", wired construction. Part of the nickeled grill, 4" series introduced in 1933. B

T-505 TRUCK WITH WRECKING CRANE, 12 1/2", circa 1931-1932. Note the screw holding the boom is mounted in the rearmost of two mounting holes, positioning the boom one inch further back in the truck pictured. The Kilgore catalog lists the truck as being 11 1/2". G

T-20 TRACTOR, 3", circa 1920s-1932. A

Kilgore states in their 1933 catalog that they were "the first to introduce genuine rubber tires on small iron toys, the first to offer iron toys in contrasting color combinations and the first to have pioneered from the beginning realism and exactitude in design."

They went on to say that "a notable achievement for this year is the presentation of Kilgore opalescent finish in an array of charming color combinations—beautiful pearly greens, reds, blues, etc. reflecting light rays as a shimmering opal."

T-486 OH BOY TRACTOR, 6", circa 1931-1932. This delicate toy, when found, generally doesn't have its rubber treads and is usually broken. F

A page from the 1931 Kilgore catalog showing some of their small tractors.

35 STEAM SHOVEL, 3 1/4", circa 1933. It is not known how long these toys were produced. These tiny steam shovels came with rubber treads, but most have gotten brittle and disintegrated. B

T-82 TRACTOR AND ROAD ROLLER, 3 3/4", circa 1931-1932.
Part of a series of tractors with attached implements. A

T-83 TRACTOR AND ROAD SCOOP, 3 1/4", circa 1931-1932. A

T-80 TRACTOR, 3", circa 1931-1932. This
tractor also came with rubber treads. A

32 CRANE TRACTOR, 4", circa 1933. It is not known when production ceased. B

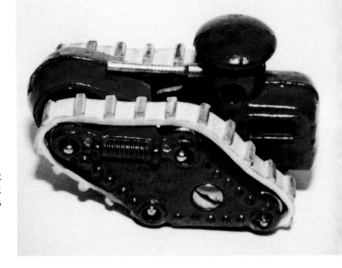

34 ARMY TANK, 2 1/2", circa 1933. It is not known when production ceased. This tank comes with an automatic movable turret gun. B

AIRPLANES

25 AIRPLANE-N4, 4 1/4", circa 1933; T-5 BULLET AIRPLANE, 3 3/4", circa 1930-1932, "Kilgore" is found in raised letters under one wing; AIRPLANE, 4 1/2", pusher type of airplane similar to the larger Sea Gull Plane. B; B; C

T-5 AIRPLANE, 3 3/4", circa 1930s. B

T-70 SEA GULL AMPHIBIAN AIRPLANE, 8", circa 1930-
1932. This is a faithful copy of Fokker's Amphibian Plane. E

T-501 TAT AIRPLANE, 11", circa 1930-1932. The TAT or Trans
Atlantic Transport Plane is modeled after a Fokker Trimotor. H

Kilgore made a limited line of boys' and girls' toys. Many of these toys were sold in Billy Boy or Sally Ann Play sets, which generally consisted of five small toys packed in a cardboard box. Several catalogs from the 1920s and the early 1930s are known to have survived.

*BILLY BOY ACCESSORY SET is a set of ten roadside accessories. F

6. VINDEX

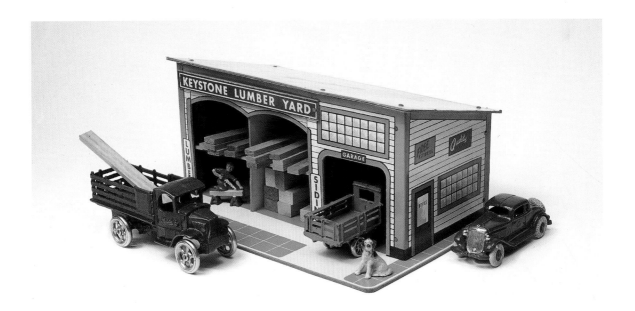

The National Sewing Machine Company of Belvedere, Illinois, produced a line of cast iron toys under the name Vindex. The name came from a special line of sewing machines produced by the company at about the same time.

The company was founded first as the Domestic Sewing Machine Company in Detroit. In 1874 the company merged and became the June Manufacturing Company, moving its headquarters to Chicago. Labor troubles caused the company to move to Belvedere, Illinois, where it would remain. In 1890 the name was changed to the National Sewing Machine Company. By 1894 the company was manufacturing more than 400 machines a year. In the same year the company diversified and began to manufacture bicycles. It even produced its own automobile, the Eldredge Runabout.

The company is believed to have begun to produce toys during the late 1920s in response to declining demand for bicycles and sewing machines. The company also produced a line of toy banks and other novelties and negotiated with Pontiac and Oldsmobile to copy their cars in miniature. Vindex also made two models of motorcycles, a P and H Power Shovel, and a complete line of John Deere and Case farm machinery. The company made a series of door stops, a bulldog bank, and an owl bank.

The company ceased its toy production in the late 1930s. After the war the company resumed production of sewing machines and washing machines. In 1948 the company merged with a California Group and became the Free Sewing Machine Company. By 1955 the company was liquidated and the foundry was sold. In its heyday, fifty of its 1500 workers were employed making toys.

AUTOMOBILES

31 OLDSMOBILE SEDAN, 8", late 1920s. Like most of the Vindex autos, the detail of their castings is great but the wheels always seem a little small. Vindex autos are scarce items. I

1 "MIKE THE SPEED COP," 8 1/2", late 1920s. Called a "true replica of the famous Excelsior-Henderson motorcycle." In the Vindex catalog this cycle is in the same size scale as the large Hubley cycles. Mike is removable. H

TRUCKS

6 STAKE TRUCK, 9 1/2", late 1920s. This truck was made in two smaller sizes. H

64 AUTOCAR DUMP TRUCK, 8", late 1920s. Like most Vindex trucks, this great looking Autocar truck is very scarce. I

VINDEX TOYS

AUTOCAR DUMP TRUCK AND CRANE

COLORS

RED, BLUE, GREEN

Loose end gate. Hoist and crank colored different than bodies. Nickel-plated wheels. Packed one in a carton, twelve to a case. Shipping wt. 2½ lbs. each. Length, 8½"; width, 3¾"; height, 4".

TOY NO. 65

Price $15.00 a dozen

AUTOCAR DUMP TRUCK

COLORS

RED, BLUE, GREEN

Loose end gate. Spring release lever dumps load. Nickel-plated wheels. Packed one in a box, twelve to a case. Shipping weight, 2½ pounds each. Length, 8½"; width, 3¾"; height, 4".

TOY NO. 64

Price $12.00 a dozen

A page from a Vindex catalog.

70 P & H POWER EXCAVATOR, 14", late
1920s to early 1930s. This shovel and
boom raise and dump by a crank. The
body can also be turned by a crank. H

FARM EQUIPMENT

36 J.L. CASE TRACTOR, 7", late 1920s to early 1930s. The toy
pictured was given to a little girl for her birthday. She liked dolls and
never played with it. It has a nickel plated driver and flywheel. G

74 CASE SPREADER, 9 1/4", late 1920s to early 1930s. Beater revolves by spring
drive. Farm Toy collectors love Vindex toys because of their realistic details. G

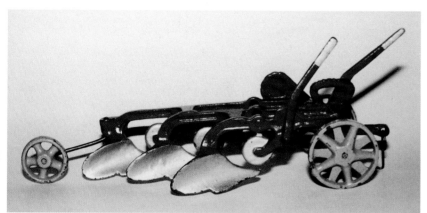

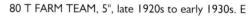

80 T FARM TEAM, 5", late 1920s to early 1930s. E

37 CASE 3-BOTTOM TRACTOR PLOW, 10 1/4", late 1920s to early 1930s. F

Pages from a 1930s catalog.

Ironically, although Vindex toys were among the more expensively priced cast iron toys, the company decided to promote them by offering them free with a special promotion with a magazine subscription to *Farm Mechanics*. "Toy Miniatures of the machines you use on your farm." Children were offered their choice of a free Vindex toy of a John Deere or Case tractor or farm equipment free with a three-year subscription of *Farm Mechanics* for the regular price of $1.00.

88 JOHN DEERE THRESHER, 15", late 1920s-early 1930s. This toy has a removable straw stacker and grain pipe. It has a nickel plated pulley. H

84 JOHN DEERE 3-BOTTOM TRACTOR PLOW, 9", late 1920s to early 1930s. F

80 JOHN DEERE FARM WAGON, 7 1/2" (not including shaft), late 1920s to early 1930s. This exact reproduction of the John Deere wagon has a removable box and seat. The running gear is quite detailed. F

89 HAY RACK, 8 1/2", late 1920s to early 1930s. The Vindex catalog states that the "hay rack fits running gear of Toy No. 80 Wagon." E

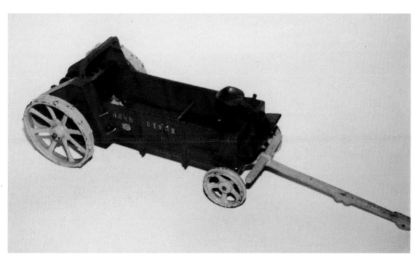

83 JOHN DEERE MANURE SPREADER, 9 1/4", late 1920s to early 1930s. The catalog calls it a "real operating toy replica of a Deere spreader." G

86 JOHN DEERE COMBINE, 16", late 1920s to early 1930s. This is a super toy. It weighs 11 pounds. The cutter and reel operate. It has imitation motor exhaust and a removable man. I

82 JOHN DEERE VAN BRUNT DRILL, 9 3/4" wide, late 1920s to early 1930s. The drill discs are nickel plated. G

Another view.

79 JOHN DEERE GAS ENGINE, 5", late 1920s to early 1930s. E

7. A.C. Williams

The A.C. Williams Company was founded in 1844 in Chagrin Falls by John W. Williams, the father of A.C. Williams, and manufactured iron castings for plow points, pump reels and spouts, wagon wheel boxes, and wheel hubs. From 1860 to 1870 the company mainly provided seamless wagon skeins and bolster plates. Williams got a contract for Cannon Carriages which were used by the government during the Civil War and forged wrought iron axles for horse-drawn carriages. Later he branched out and began to produce pruning tools.

The original factory was built in 1844 in Chagrin Falls and then rebuilt in 1890 after a 1889 fire. In 1890 fire again struck and the company moved to Ravenna, Ohio, where it built another factory and continued to produce hardware, house furnishings, cast iron objects, and cast iron toys. Company brochures advertised that the company produced light gray iron, semi-steel, magnesium castings and hardware.

During the first World War the company's Gray Iron Foundry made many vital products in connection with the war effort. The company shipped its products nationwide due to its central location and its direct connections with the Pennsylvania, the Baltimore and Ohio, and the Erie Railroads.

Williams made toys during the 1920s and 1930s but production ceased by the second World War. The company probably made more smaller-sized vehicles than any other company and sold them through five and ten cent stores.

*TOURING CAR, 9 1/4", 1920s. This toy is the largest of two sizes and has wonderful nickel plated wheels showing the brake drum behind the spokes. Generally called a Lincoln by collectors, it is certainly one of the nicest toys made by Williams. F

268 COUPE, 3 3/4", early 1930s. Came with nickel plated wheels. B

5-T COUPE, 6 1/2", early 1930s. The details of this Coupe with its nickel plated rumble seat are very nicely executed. It also came in a larger size. D

8067 FORD COUPE, 4 1/4", late 1920s to 1930s. B

*COUPE, 5", 1930s. The body is held to the chassis
by a spring clip and can be removed. C

*SEDAN, 5", 1930s. The body is held to the
chassis by a spring clip and can be removed. C

62-T CHRYSLER, 6 3/4"; 57-T CHRYSLER, 4 3/4". Both late 1930s. These two toys have a single casting body attached to a nickel plated chassis by a spring clip. Like many of the toys made in the mid to late 1930s that have nickel plated grills, they are hard to find today. D; C

73-T PACKARD SEDAN, 6 3/4", late 1930s. This toy was made as a single piece casting resulting in limited detail. It is somewhat difficult to find. D

From a 1937 supplement to A.C. Williams catalog #51.

70-T FORD ROADSTER, 4 1/4", about 1937. This is a very desirable A.C. Williams toy. It came with a nickel plated windshield, grill, headlights, and chassis. It is very scarce. E

568 SAFETY COACH, 3 1/2". A

9467 TWIN COACH, 5", late 1920s to mid 1930s. Came in four colors with nickel plated wheels. B

4-T RACER, 4", early 1930s. Made in four sizes, this racer has a driver and mechanic. This is the smallest size yet it still is nicely detailed. B

468 AUTO RACER, 3 1/2", 1930s. A

TRUCKS

W 88 TRUCK WITH STAKE BODY TRAILER, 5 1/2"; 168 MACK AUTO TRUCK, 3 1/2". Both 1930s. C; B

5767 FORD TRUCK, 7", 1920s. This toy has rather unusual wheels which are made from two steel stampings. D

58 DUMP CAR TRAILER, 3 1/2", early 1930s. This toy also came in a 4 1/2" size that was available into the mid 1930s. A

8367 ROAD SCRAPER, 4 1/2", late 1920s to mid 1930s. Came with nickel plated wheels and in three sizes. This one is the smallest. B

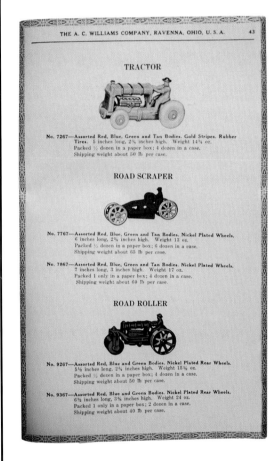

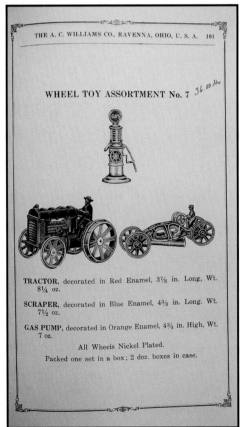

Two pages from an A.C. Williams catalog.

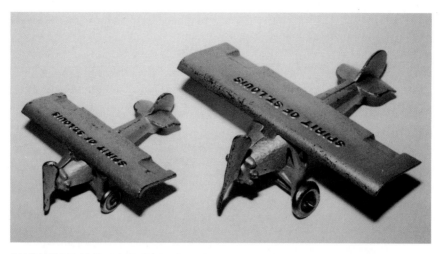

9667 AEROPLANE, 4 1/2"; 9767 AEROPLANE, 5 3/4". These two airplanes were apparently made only for a couple of years and are not easily found. They appear in the 49th edition catalog, which is believed to have been issued in 1929. C; D

1168 AEROPLANE, 3 3/4", early to mid 1930s. Has nickel plated wheels and propeller. B

9667 AEROPLANE, 4 1/2", early to mid 1930s. Came with nickel plated motor, wheels, and propeller. Has the same catalog number as the earlier version shown above. C

4967 AUTO RACER, 5 1/2 ", late 1920s. C

8. Other Cast Iron Toy Manufacturers

CHAMPION

The Champion Safety Lock Company was founded in 1883 in a small Ohio town named Geneva, just a few miles outside Cleveland, by John A. and Ezra Hasenpflug. Its first successful product was a special piece of hardware used to lock windows in partly opened positions. In 1902 the company bought a larger building and expanded its production. In 1911 the company was renamed the Champion Hardware Company and three years later established its own iron foundry. In 1924 the Hasenpflugs sold out their interests in the company to C.I. Chamberlin.

By 1930 the company had lost many of its former contract work and began to look for more outlets. It was then that Chamberlin and the board of directors decided to produce a line of cast iron toys. Champion toys were sold mostly through chain and variety stores.

Champion produced toys for around six years and finally ceased its toy production in 1936 and returned to manufacturing builders' hardware full time. The company filled government contracts throughout World War II and returned to the hardware business after the war. In 1954 the company was acquired and merged into Washington Steel Products.

*AIRFLOW SEDAN, 4 3/4", mid 1930s. Attributed to Champion. Has a nickel plated grill that is so loose fitting that it is frequently missing. C

530 CHAMPION COUPE, 7 1/4", mid 1930s. This is a very well designed toy with an opening rumble seat and a nickel plated grill. It sure looks like a 1933 Plymouth. F

542 AUTO SEDAN, 4 1/2", early to mid 1930s. B

550 AUTO RACER with DRIVER, 6", early to mid 1930s. Has a separate driver held in place by the rear axle. C

536 CHAMPION DELIVERY
TRUCK, 8", early to mid 1930s. E

GLOBE

3012 AUTOMOBILE WITH DRIVER AND PASSENGERS,
12", early 1930s. The Globe catalog notes that "this toy is
painted in a beautiful shade of green, and comes complete
with driver and two passengers in rumble seat." It is
equipped with imitation motor exhaust sound and spare
tire. The hood ornament resembles an Indian. This toy is
very scarce. H

3000 FIRE CHIEF CAR, 12", early 1930s. Like #3012 this car has a rumble seat (although this one is without passengers), a separate driver, a spare tire, and an imitation motor exhaust sound. The bumper was a separate casting. H

Little information is known about Globe Toys. We found only one mention of Globe Toys in a 1931 Edward K. Tryon Company catalog. Tryon was a sporting goods store in Philadelphia. The catalog listed eight toys including the 3040 Motorcycle with Officer pictured below. Also included were the 3012 Automobile with Driver and Passengers, the 3020 Cannon and Soldiers, and the 3030 Racing Car.

3040 POLICE MOTORCYCLE, 8 1/2", mid 1930s. This motorcycle looks much like a Hubley cycle until you discover that it has a cast-in driver and other features that make it different. It was made by Globe, a little known manufacturer that apparently only existed for a brief period and made but a handful of models. G

This toy retailed for $1.00 in 1931. The catalog description notes that the "officer is in regulation uniform. The motorcycle is painted bright red. Imitation motor exhaust. Real rubber tires. Packed one in a heavy corrugated carton." There is also a note that the standard shipping package contains 12 toys—approximate weight 28 lbs. Another motorcycle, the 3045 Motorcycle with Officer and Side Car, is also shown. The catalog listing says that the "officer finished to look natural in blue uniform."

The Grey Iron Toy company was founded in the 1880s in Mount Joy, Pennsylvania. Little else is known about the company.

*COUPE, 8", 1920s. This toy was also made in a smaller size and is often thought to be a reproduction. C

100 GREY IRON TRAFFIC SIGNAL, 9 1/4" h., 1930s. A battery contained in the base supplies the current to power the red and green signals. A lever rotates the top from "stop" to "go." E

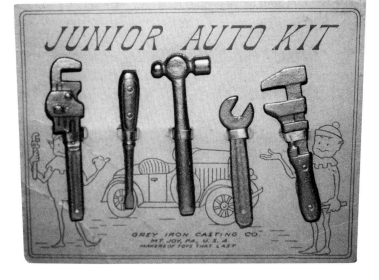

*GREY IRON JUNIOR AUTO KIT, 5 3/4" wide, 1930s. Several makers of cast iron toys produced small tools like this Grey Iron kit and they are fairly easy to find. However, not many can be found still attached to the card. B

*GREY IRON MIDGET AUTO SET, 1938. This set retailed for 5 cents and contained five cast iron 1 1/2" vehicles. B

*GREY IRON MIDGET AUTO SET, 8 1/4", late 1930s. This is probably a prototype set that may never have reached production. The box appears to be hand-made and lettered. C

FREIDAG

In 1920 William F. Freidag (sometimes pronounced Friday) founded the Freidag Manufacturing Company in Freeport, Illinois, just five blocks north of another toy company, the Arcade Manufacturing Company. The company occupied a dismantled World War I army barracks and at one time had more than 240 workers and boasted that they had the largest foundry floor space in Freeport. The company made among other products, grey iron, brass, aluminum, and iron castings for automobile accessories, cement mixers, coffee mills, waffle irons, lamps, golf clubs, and cast iron and aluminum toys.

"Freeport, Illinois is fast becoming known as the manufacturing center for toys as it is the home of the Freidag Mfg Co., Arcade Mfg Co. the Structo Mfg Co and the S.N. Swan & Sons Co.," stated an article in the trade magazine *Playthings*, adding that "the company's best toy was a Double Decker Fifth Avenue Bus." The company also carried a line of cabs—the Yellow Cab, the Checkered Cab, and the Black and White Cab.

They made a nice series of 8-inch Chevrolet trucks. It has been noted that many of the Freidag toys were similar to

*TAXI, 5 1/4", 1920s. This taxi has a separate spare tire with license plate "543." D

those made by Arcade. The Yellow Cab, which was one of Arcade's biggest sellers, was also the biggest seller for Freidag. After the Depression the Freidag Company was forced to close and William Freidag went to work for Arcade.

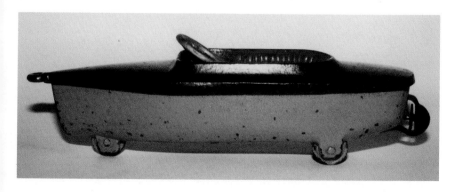

*MOTORBOAT, 10 1/4", 1920s. We have not found another motorboat like this. E

229

*DOUBLE DECKER BUS, 9", 1930s. This somewhat boxy looking toy has separate castings of passengers riveted to each side of the bus. F

Detail.

NORTH AND JUDD

North and Judd was a small cast iron company located in New Britain, Connecticut. Only about four or five North and Judd toys are known to exist and little information is known about the company's production. We have not been able to locate any catalogs for the company.

*AMERICAN BANTAM ROADSTER, 3 1/2", 1930s. E

NIEDERST

*NIEDERST STEAM SHOVEL, 20". This large all cast iron steam shovel was made by the Niederst Company of Chicago, Illinois. On each side in raised letters are the words "Good Roads Machinery Toys." It is perhaps the largest cast iron automotive toy ever manufactured and only two have come to light. I

UNKNOWN MANUFACTURERS

*ROADSTER, 8 1/2", mid 1930s. Maker unknown. This toy hasn't been found in any catalogs and is a very rare toy. It has a look of an Auburn. F

*COUPE, 8 1/4", mid 1930s. The manufacturer of this sleek coupe with its long hood and graceful fenders, like its near twin Roadster, is unknown. F

PART THREE: BUILDINGS, GAS STATIONS, AND SIGNAGE

Cast iron toy companies not only produced miniature vehicles, they also manufactured miniature cast iron gas pumps, road signs, and motor accessories. Just as little girls liked to play with doll houses so little boys enjoyed filling up their cars and trucks at "play" service stations, flying their planes in "play" airports, and driving up to "drive-in" restaurants. Usually these buildings were made out of wood, masonite, steel, and cardboard, and were made to scale with the majority of the cast iron cars, truck, and motorcycles. Arcade was one of the manufacturers of these realistic miniature buildings. In the 1930s the Pure Oil Company sold models of their uniquely styled gas station buildings as promotions. One Pure Station model was also a birdhouse. Another was a radio. Gibbs was another toy company that made these "toy" service stations.

Richtoy, Keystone, and Schoenhut as well as many other companies also made toy gas stations, firehouses, airports, and houses. However Arcade was the only cast iron toy maker to make wooden buildings.

ARCADE STREET SIGNS, 1938-1941. Most signs were sold in sets with other toys and were not sold individually. A

ARCADE STREET SIGNS. These are known as the round base signs and were made from about 1924 to 1936. They are more difficult to find then the later tri-foot base variety. B

*ARCADE NCR '41 SIGN. This was probably made by Arcade for a National Cash Register Company event in 1941. C

331 ARCADE TRAFFIC ASSORTMENT, 1933. The price tag from H. Snellenburgs in Philadelphia is for $.95 cents. G

*ARCADE TROPICAL PAINT COMPANY SIGN. This sign would have been a special order item from Arcade probably from around 1935. C

*LINCOLN HIGHWAY SIGN. Lincoln Highway is Route 30 and when it was built in 1923, it was the first United States cross-country highway. A

929 ARCADE SIGNBOARD, wood. This billboard was offered by Arcade primarily for dealers' display in the late 1920s and early 1930s. E

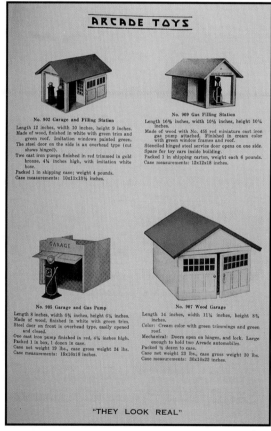

A page from an Arcade catalog.

447 ARCADE MCCORMICK-DEERING CREAM SEPARATOR, 4 7/8" h., 1932-1936. D

906 ARCADE GARAGE, 8" l., 1933-1936. Has a steel overhead door. E

896 ARCADE FIRE ENGINE HOUSE, 12" wide, 1941. This wood building came with two cast iron Pontiac fire trucks. F (with fire trucks)

909 ARCADE GAS FILLING STATION, 16 5/8" l., 1933-1936. Came with one cast iron gas pump. F

ARCADE GAS STATION.

907 ARCADE TOY WOOD
GARAGE, 14" l., 1930-1936. E

A RICH TOY GARAGE. This company made several toy garages in the
1930s. The buildings are made of wood and pressboard. C

A RICH TOY SKYWAY AIRPORT. C

A RICH TOY GARAGE. C

A RICH TOY SIGN. A

RICH PLAY BUILDING. Drive-ins became popular in the 1940s. Curb Service was the selling point. C

Another RICH SERVICE STATION. C

897 ARCADIA AIRPORT, 12" wide, 1941. This building was made of wood and came with two Arcade 3630 airplanes. F (with airplanes)

900 ARCADE FILLING STATION, 12 1/2" long, 1940. The building and floor are wood. It came with a cast iron gas pump island and a steel grease rack. D

A plain ARCADE GARAGE with TWO GAS PUMPS.

902 ARCADE GARAGE AND FILL-ING STATION, 12" l., 1936-1940. Came with two cast iron red gas pumps and a steel overhead door. The building was made of wood. F

*GO SIGN, 5" h., 1925. Probably made by Arcade for a special event. C

Left and below:
These were promotional items that were probably given out at the Buick dealerships during the 1920s/1930s. They were nice 'go-withs' for cast iron vehicles. B

453 "ARCADE GAS" PUMP, 6 1/4" h., 1926-1931. This pump did not come with a hose. D

ARCADE GAS PUMP.

455 ARCADE GAS
PUMP, 6" h., 1932-1936.
D

456 ARCADE GAS PUMP
BANK, 5 3/4" h., 1936. D

70 KILGORE GAS PUMP, 6 1/4" h.,
1927. This Kilgore gas pump is one
of the most difficult cast iron pumps
to find. D

8567 A. C. WILLIAMS GAS
PUMPS, 4 3/4" h., 1930s.
(Note both side crank and
rear crank versions.) C

8667 A.C. WILLIAMS GAS
PUMP, 6 3/4" h., 1930s. D

SERVICE STATION, circa 1940s-
1950s. Maker unknown. B

Above and right:
298 DENT AIR MAIL BANK, 6 1/4" h.. D

288 DENT STOP AND SAVE
BANKS, 5 3/4" and 4 1/2" h. C

PURE GAS STATION BIRD HOUSE
with a Kilgore car parked in front. D

A PURE GAS STATION
RADIO. The cord,
controls, and speakers
are in the rear. F

Gibbs was an Ohio toy company that made buildings such as this one. The two
cars are "mystery cars." No one seems to know who made them. D

A recent Bill Weart/Jim Levengood garage.

Maker unknown. B

Richtoy freight office. B

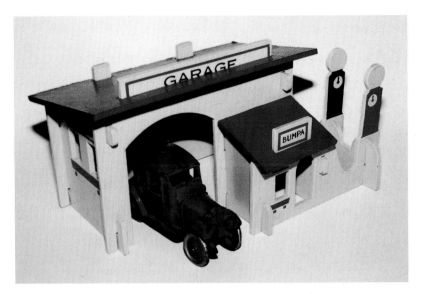

Bumpalow garage. B

Schoenhut garage.D

Part Four: Researching Your Toys: Using Catalogs

1. Catalogs and Fold Outs

While a few cast iron toys were made in Great Britain and Sweden during the beginning of the twentieth century, the majority of these toys were made in the United States, by eight companies.

Dating cast iron toys is not an exact science. We have tried to be as accurate as possible in our dates and have researched all available manufacturers' catalogs in order to do so. Unfortunately not all companies issued a new catalog every year or on a regular basis. Cast iron toy catalogs were printed in very small numbers and were intended to be used as a tool to sell the toys at a wholesale level. They were given to purchasing agents for retail stores and not intended to be used by the public. This is the reason that so few exist today. By comparison, Lionel, the electric train manufacturer, printed millions of retail catalogs and many original catalogs exist today.

Whenever we could, we researched as many catalogs as possible to trace each year of a toy's production. We believe we were successful with regard to Arcade, Hubley, and Kenton. In other instances we were able to date the toy according to a time range such as "early 1920s." However, in some cases we were not able to find any specific dates for a toy at all and had to deduce a date using other clues such as the years of production for the actual car or truck or make an educated guess. Most toys had a specific production run and were produced every year for a certain time period. However, there are those toys for which the manufacture was erratic where a toy was made for a few years, production suspended, and then the toy reintroduced years later.

Arcade is the best researched company. Hubley and Kenton also have been well researched. Information on Kenton can be found at the Kenton, Ohio, Historical Society. And Hubley can be researched at the Heritage Museum in Lancaster, Pennsylvania.

Dating Dent toys is difficult since there are only two existing toy catalogs for the Dent Hardware Company and neither is dated. There are some fold-out Dent catalog supplements though—"Iron and Aluminum Toys," "Toyland's Treasure Chests (boxed sets)," and "Iron Toys"—but these are not dated either. Because of the lack of information, in at-tempting to date Dent toys we used a deductive process. We do know that Dent began its production of toys in 1898 and by 1903 had produced a complete line of toys. Thus we can assume that the catalog entitled *Cast Iron Toys* is the first catalog because it only shows horse-drawn vehicles. We must also assume that the No. 10 catalog was issued after 1927 because it shows Dent's toy model of the *Lindy*, Charles Lindbergh's famous airplane, and we know that Lindbergh made his famous flight in 1927.

There are few catalogs for Kilgore, Grey Iron, Champion, and Vindex. We found one reference to Globe in a catalog from Edward H. Tryon, a Philadelphia sporting goods

Fairy Story Booklet
A limited supply of booklets are available for Arcade toy dealers. This 16-page book printed in color contains a beautiful fairy story in jingle form about Fred and Jane and their pleasant experiences with "The Tiny Arcadians," a fairy folk who, in the story, are the makers of Arcade Cast Iron Toys.

Electrotypes and newspaper mats on all toy items gladly supplied without charge.

BRANCH OFFICES

NEW YORK	CHICAGO
200 Fifth Avenue	Merchandise Mart
Room 415	Room 14111

REPRESENTATIVE OFFICES

PHILADELPHIA	BOSTON
D. H. Youngs	A. T. Otis
6146 Wayne Avenue	111 Summer Street
MEMPHIS	ATLANTA
Orgill & Dwyer Co.	A. G. Brennan
Clay-Tate Bldg.	20 Ivy Street
DALLAS	SAN FRANCISCO
D. D. Otstott Co.	Erlach-Lee Co.
727 Santa Fe Bldg.	718 Mission Street

store. We found no catalogs for North and Judd, the small toy company in New Britain, Connecticut.

It is interesting to note that for many years during the first part of the twentieth century, Pennsylvania and Ohio were the centers for the manufacture of cast iron toys. In addition to the Hubley and the Dent companies, three other companies made cast iron toys in Pennsylvania—William Shimer and Son, Grey Iron, and Jones & Bixler. Ohio was the home of Kenton, Kilgore, A.C. Williams, and Champion, and Arcade, Vindex, and Freidag were located in Illinois.

In the beginning years of the industry most companies distributed their own toy lines to individual stores, but gradually they realized the need for national distribution and hired agents who were based in New York, Chicago, and other major American cities.

During the pre-World War II days, the owners of the leading companies were friends, met often to exchange ideas, and attended national meetings together. Richard Dent remembers his grandfather traveling with Ives, Hubley, and other leading toy manufacturers to national conventions and meetings, and that it was not unusual for the companies to share expertise, buy their rivals' patterns, and cast parts such as wheels for another company's toys.

1929 ARCADE catalog cover.

1932 ARCADE catalog cover.

1926 ARCADE catalog cover.

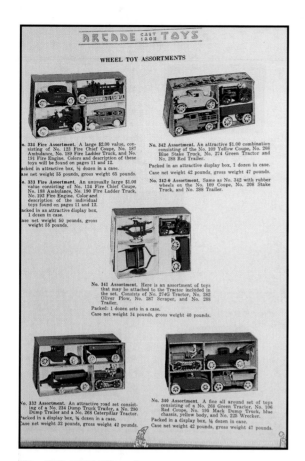

The 1932 ARCADE catalog
shows some of their boxed sets.

The 1936 ARCADE catalog cover.

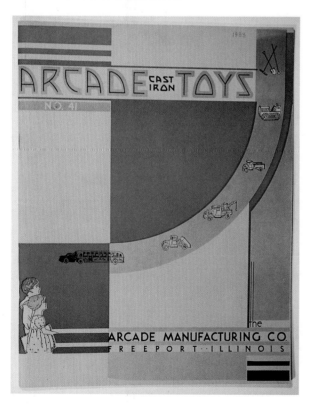

1933 ARCADE catalog cover.

1940 ARCADE catalog cover.

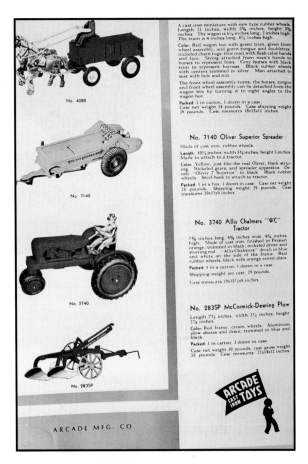

A page from an ARCADE catalog
showing farm equipment.

From the cover of an ARCADE 1925 catalog.

A page from *The Young Arcadians*, showing children playing with
a firetruck, Andy Gump car, taxi, and a policeman.

Box lid from a 1930s Road Building Set.

The cover of a 1929 ARCADE catalog.

This was a time when individual toys were cherished and seemed to have greater meaning to children than toys do today when children have so many and toys seem to be disposable.

The "Young Arcadians" showed many of the most popular ARCADE toys.

A page from a pamphlet that ARCADE
produced to elicit interest in its line of toys.

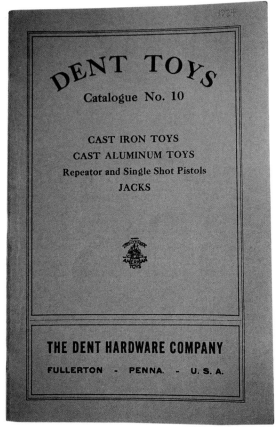

The DENT no. 10 catalog.

ARCADE produced many novelties
such as this Circus Wagon.

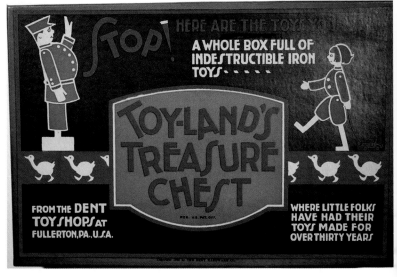

A box from a 1928 Toyland Treasure Chest set.

Cover of a DENT Road-Builder set box.

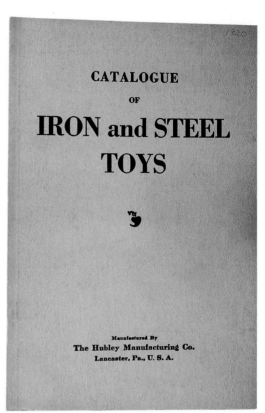

1920 HUBLEY catalog cover.

The 1928 HUBLEY catalog cover.

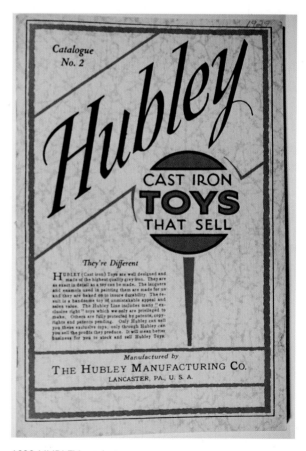

1929 HUBLEY catalog cover.

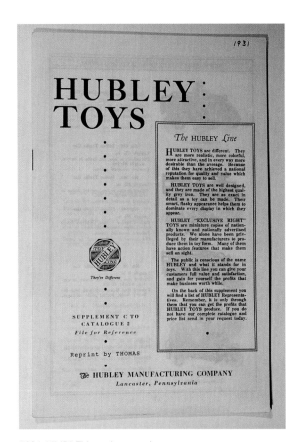

1931 HUBLEY catalog supplement cover.

1933 HUBLEY catalog supplement cover.

1932 HUBLEY catalog cover.

1936 HUBLEY catalog cover.

1938 HUBLEY catalog cover.

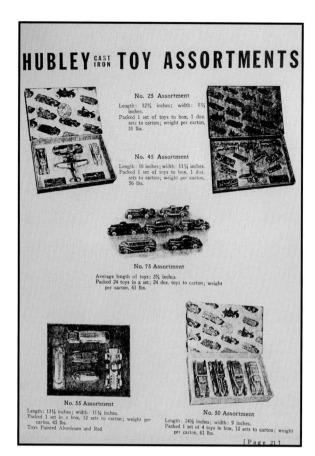

A page from the 1938 HUBLEY catalog showing several of their boxed sets.

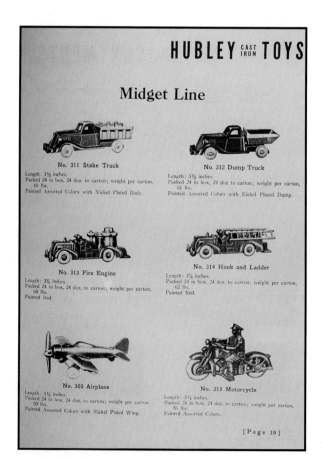

A page from the 1938 HUBLEY catalog showing part the company's Midget Line of Cast Iron Toys.

The 1940 HUBLEY catalog cover.

255

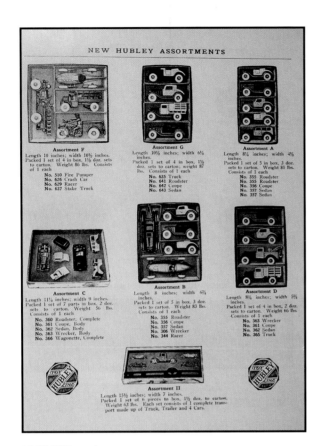

HUBLEY boxed sets.

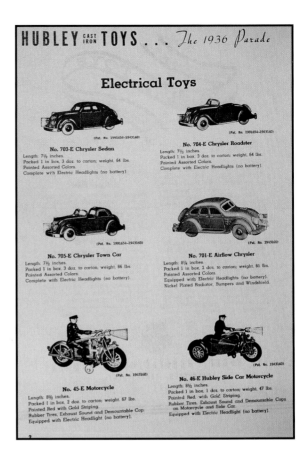

A page from a HUBLEY catalog showing its electrical toys. These electrical toys were only produced for a few years.

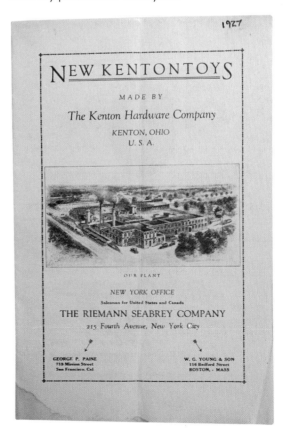

The cover of the 1927 KENTON supplement.

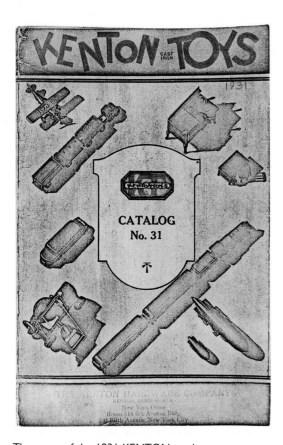

The cover of the 1931 KENTON catalog.

From the 1940 KENTON folder.

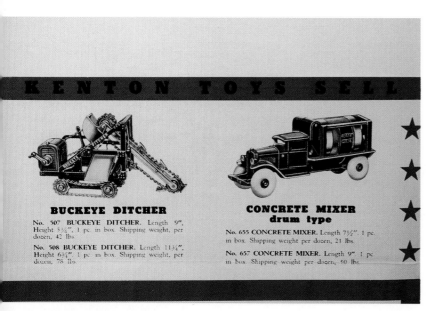

From the 1940 KENTON folder.

Cover of the 1931 KILGORE catalog.

257

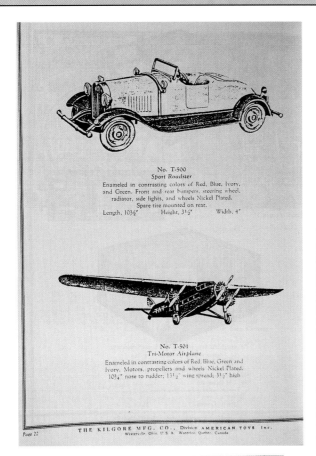

No. T-500
Sport Roadster
Enameled in contrasting colors of Red, Blue, Ivory,
and Green. Front and rear bumpers, steering wheel,
radiator, side lights, and wheels Nickel Plated.
Spare tire mounted on rear.
Length, 10½"   Height, 3½"   Width, 4"

No. T-501
Tri-Motor Airplane
Enameled in contrasting colors of Red, Blue, Green and
Ivory. Motors, propellers and wheels Nickel Plated.
10¾" nose to rudder; 13½" wing spread; 3½" high

Page 22   THE KILGORE MFG. CO., Division AMERICAN TOYS Inc.
Westerville, Ohio, U.S.A. Waterloo, Quebec, Canada

A page from a KILGORE catalog.

Page from the 1939 GREY IRON TOYS catalog.

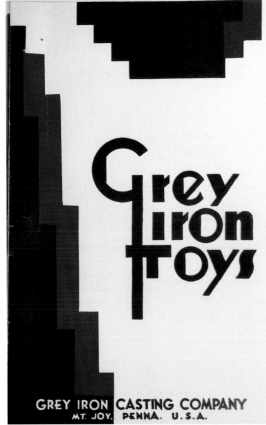

The cover of a 1939 GREY IRON TOYS catalog.

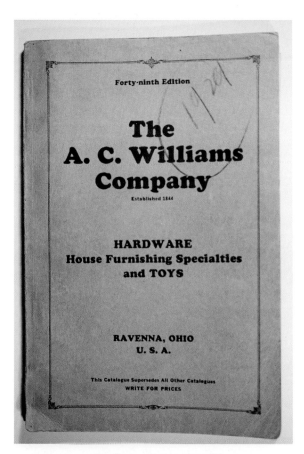

The cover of a 1929 A.C. WILLIAMS catalog.

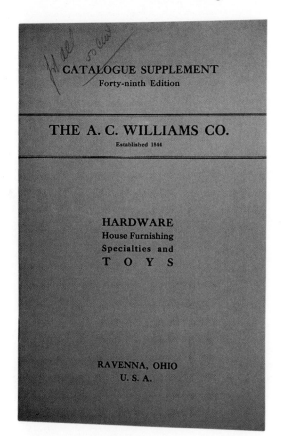

The cover of a supplement to the
1929 A. C. WILLIAMS catalog.

The cover of a 1934 A.C. WILLIAMS catalog.

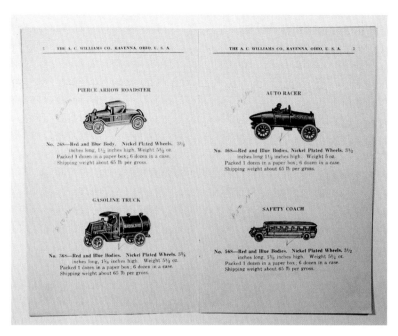

Page from the A.C. WILLIAMS 1929 catalog supplement.

A page from the 1934 A.C. WILLIAMS catalog.

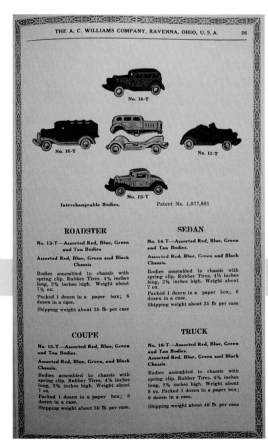

A page from the 1934 A.C.
WILLIAMS catalog.

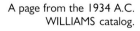

260

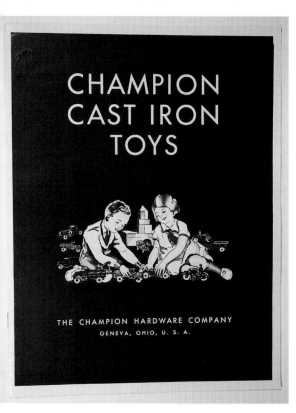

Cover of a mid 1930s CHAMPION catalog.

No. 538 and No. 438

From the CHAMPION catalog.

From the CHAMPION catalog.

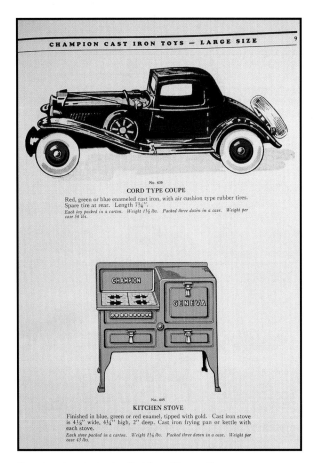

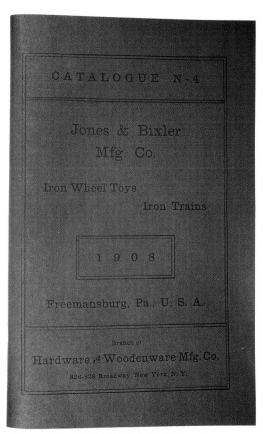

Showing the nicely detailed "cord" type Coupe.

Cover of the 1908 JONES & BIXLER catalog showing some of the very scarce early autos. All of these cars are very difficult to find today.

JONES & BIXLER only made toys for a few years in the early 1900s.

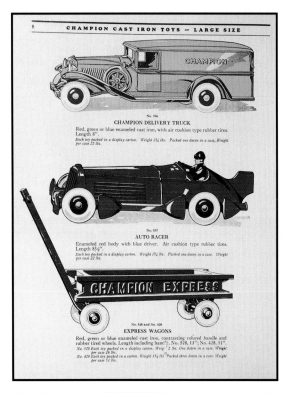

Page showing three CHAMPION cast iron toys.

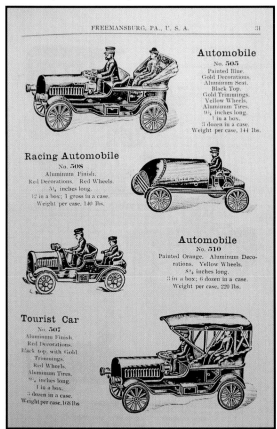

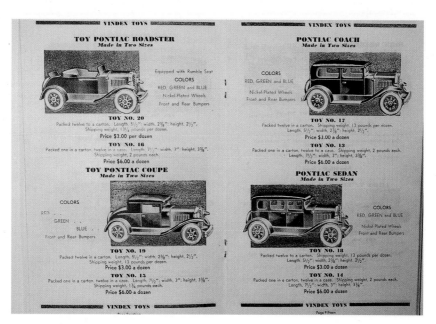

From an early 1930s VINDEX catalog.

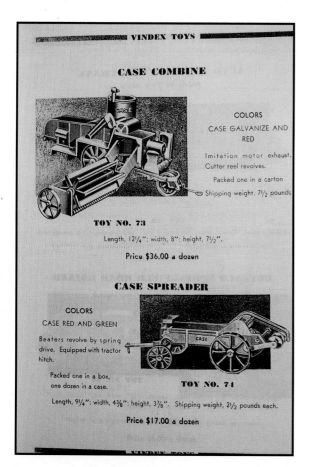

From an early 1930s VINDEX catalog.

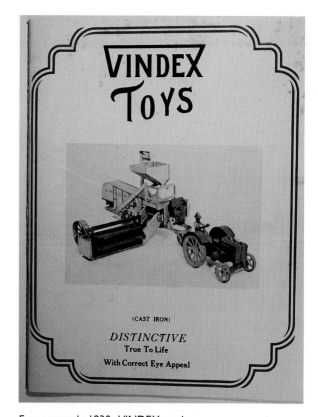

From an early 1930s VINDEX catalog.

Advertising Dolls. Myra Yellin Outwater. Dolls not only capture little girls' hearts, they've also managed to corner markets for mega-companies like W.K. Kellogg Company, Jolly Green Giant, and Campbell's. The author has scoured flea markets and auction houses and consumed cereals, candies, and innumerable hamburgers in order to compile one of the most complete collections of advertising dolls known to exist.

This comprehensive book traces the emergence of dolls like Aunt Jemima and Betty Crocker, who leant their stamp of domestic credibility, and chronicles the extraordinary rise of figures like Ronald McDonald and the California Raisins, tiny figures which invaded homes and helped define American culture. Here is the nostalgic revisit of hundreds of advertising creations, like Uneeda Kid, Buddy Lee, Cracker Jack, Charlie Tuna, Burger King, and Trix the Rabbit. Each is shown with front and back details, and current values are listed providing the perfect reference tool for the collector.

Size: 8 1/2" x 11"   498 color photos   Price Guide   160pp.
ISBN: 0-7643-0303-1   soft cover $29.95

Ocean Liner Collectibles. Myra Yellin Outwater. This book recreates the ambiance of the ocean liner era by showing the actual objects used on board. Each piece of ocean liner memorabilia is like an Aladdin's lamp, releasing wondrous memories of that grand style of travel. Beginning in the late 1890s, shipping lines forged their identities by commissioning unique furniture, china, silverware, glassware, vases, ashtrays, playing cards, menus, and stationery. These types of items characterized the different ocean liners, from the Normandie with her elegant Art Deco furnishings, to the stainless steel gleam of the S.S. United States, to the old-world luxury of the Queens.

Size: 8 1/2" x 11"   585 color photos   Price Guide   160pp.
ISBN: 0-7643-0581-6   soft cover $29.95

Florida Kitsch. Myra & Eric Outwater. Florida is the land of pink flamingoes, bathing beauties, palm trees, coconuts, and beaches. It is a tourist mecca and a treasure trove of souvenirs. This book is a salute to the popular Florida tourist culture of the 1940s through the 1970s, when mostly northern tourists embraced the Florida sun and beaches with open arms, discovering along with Florida's natural beauty, a lot of kooky kitsch. Kitsch is colorful, funky, fun, and collectible. This book, with its 250 photos, remembers the nostalgic, whimsical objects often bought on impulse, brought home as gifts or mementos, and then relegated to shelves, attics, and bathrooms to sit for years, undusted, as visible reminders of happy trips. Whether a native

of Florida, a seasonal visitor, or one in need of a getaway, this book is sure to evoke a bit of Florida sunshine for all.
Size: 11" x 8 1/2"   247 color photos   112pp.
                                          Price Guide/Index
ISBN: 0-7643-0944-7   soft cover $19.95

Judaica. Myra Yellin Outwater. Photography by Eric B. Outwater. Judaica embraces those objects associated with the celebration of and adherence to Jewish rituals. This book presents clear explanations and beautiful color pictures of candlesticks, boxes, plates, cups, toys, and foods which celebrate Jewish traditions. These objects of creative design display, honor and rekindle the spirit of a 5000-year-old religion to reflect 20th century modernism.
Size: 8 1/2" x 11"   616 color photos   192pp.
                                          Price Guide/Index
ISBN: 0-7643-0785-1   hard cover $49.95

Floridiana: Collecting Florida's Best. Myra Yellin Outwater & Eric B. Outwater. Florida is always associated with all that is bright, colorful, funky, and fun. This book captures the spirit of Florida in the collectibles, ephemera, souvenirs, and nostalgic items that it produced. There are also highlights of Florida history and its culture, a price guide, and an index. Complete with postcards, tablecloths, ceramics, clothing, jewelry, dolls, figurines, and much more, it celebrates the tourist culture that helped populate Florida from the 1900s through the 1970s. Over 650 photographs bring the fun and fantasy of Florida to life, presenting what many consider as truly Florida's best!
Size: 8 1/2" x 11"   654 color photos   Price Guide   160pp.
ISBN: 0-7643-0973-0   soft cover $29.95

Schiffer books may be ordered from your local bookstore, or they may be ordered directly from the publisher by writing to:

Schiffer Publishing Ltd.
4880 Lower Valley Road
Atglen, PA 19310
Phone: (610) 593-1777; Fax: (610) 593-2002
E-mail: Schifferbk@aol.com

Please visit our web site catalog at www.schifferbooks.com or write for a free catalog. Please include $3.95 for shipping and handling for the first two books and 50¢ for each additional book. Free shipping for orders of $100 or more.

Printed in China